T0289837

Keeping Your Business in the U.S.A.

Profit Globally While Operating Locally

Keeping Your Business in the U.S.A.
Profit Globally While Operating Locally

Tim Hutzel
Paul Piechota

CRC Press
Taylor & Francis Group
Boca Raton London New York

CRC Press is an imprint of the
Taylor & Francis Group, an **informa** business
A PRODUCTIVITY PRESS BOOK

CRC Press
Taylor & Francis Group
6000 Broken Sound Parkway NW, Suite 300
Boca Raton, FL 33487-2742

Printed in the United States of America on acid-free paper
Version Date: 20110801

International Standard Book Number: 978-1-4398-0778-1 (Hardback)

Library of Congress Cataloging-in-Publication Data

Hutzel, Tim.
    Keeping your business in the USA : profit globally while operating locally / Tim Hutzel and Paul Piechota.
        p. cm.
    Includes bibliographical references and index.
    ISBN 978-1-4398-0778-1
    1. Business enterprises--United States. 2. Success in business--United States. 3. Globalization. I. Piechota, Paul. II. Title.

HF3031.H88 2012
658.00973--dc22   2011008913

Visit the Taylor & Francis Web site at
http://www.taylorandfrancis.com

and the CRC Press Web site at
http://www.crcpress.com

To the multitude of small, medium, and large businesses that are struggling to keep their work in America.

To the many businesses that have been successful keeping their work in America whom we have learned from and were able to write this book.

To those Americans in business, academia, and government who have the Vision of making America the manufacturing superpower we once were.

To the men and women who are unemployed because work has been outsourced who will one day be employed again in meaningful jobs producing meaningful products.

To our collective grandchildren who will profit by those leaders who read—learn—understand—apply the principles in this book… Keeping Your Business in the U.S.A. Profit Globally While Operating Locally.

Contents

Foreword

My role as a county commissioner is to ensure the vitality and viability of my area of responsibility. For my constituents that means, in great deal, ensuring jobs are abundant and meaningful. The mad rush to outsource more and more manufacturing jobs to China, India, and other faraway lands has made my job very difficult.

As I see it, our country is at a crossroads. It can either take the initiative and do something constructive to rebuild American manufacturing capabilities and manufacturing centers of excellence or continue down the path of passiveness and do nothing.

I am sure most of this book's readers will agree with me that the once shiny lure of cheap labor was just that, a lure. Like the unwise fish that was attracted to the shiny lure soon discovered, only doom followed once it bit … hook, line, and sinker.

Just look at what we have become—a nation subservient to the whims and risks of countries that displaced our manufacturing might. Don't you think it is a pity that you cannot walk through a large department store without finding any more than a handful of products made in America? It is enough to make a body sit down and cry.

I, for one, will do something about this dilemma. My vision is to make Made in America a reality once again, and the retention of businesses and employees my mission. That will take legislation, incentives, hard work, but, most of all, leadership. My constituents can count on me for that; it's a promise I will not break.

As for the authors of this book, they, too, are leaders. It is from their burning passion that they decided to write *Keeping Your Business in the U.S.A.: Profit Globally While Operating Locally* and share the stories of successful American manufacturers and their firsthand experiences spanning almost 100 years.

This book can be the first step in you *Keeping Your Business* (manufacturing jobs) *in the U.S.A.*, or bringing jobs back *if* you apply the principles you find within its pages.

What I really like about *Keeping Your Business in the U.S.A.* is the way it is written. It is easy to understand, easy to know what to do, and, most importantly, will give you a leg up on keeping your jobs in America.

Dan Foley
Commissioner,
Montgomery County, Ohio

Preface

Manufacturing jobs are leaving America at a far greater rate than those coming in. Outsourcing mania has become the norm among American producers. Worse yet, entire companies are folding completely, leaving only their brand names attached to products still sold in America, but made far from American shores. Once icons, with such names as Seth Thomas, Singer, and Schwinn, are now made in China and are faint reminders of the era when American manufacturing dominated the world.

Who are we and why did we write this book? Quite frankly, we have been alarmed at the flight overseas of American manufacturing. It is a sad but true fact that American companies have been chasing cheaper labor in China, India, and other countries around the world. This has placed the citizens of the United States in a very vulnerable position. We have become overly dependent on offshore countries to manufacture our goods and products.

There are legitimate reasons for this. Formerly, "Made in America" was a badge of honor, but sometimes it meant mediocre quality and high cost. And, while America was enjoying the post World War II economic boom, the Japanese were literally rising from their ashes. With help from quality pioneers like W. Edwards Deming and supported financially by America, Japan steadily became better and better at manufacturing. As they improved, consumers noticed and began defecting from American products, small ones at first. A Yashika camera was purchased instead of an Argus, a small transistor radio "Made in Japan" was bought instead of a Philco or Crosley, which was made in the United States.

In the late 1960s, Toyota entered the American automobile market with odd little cars that seemed to run forever and caught the attention of the consumer, but with more significant money changing hands than for radios and cameras. So much money, in fact, that soon the automotive giants noticed and wanted to know more about what the Japanese were doing. American manufacturers began to learn bits and pieces of what was happening in Japan and wanted the instantaneous improvement that seemed to come with it. With a high degree of impatience and misunderstanding, most failed at trying to implement such things as quality circles and statistical process control, manufacturing tactics that were flourishing in Japan and supporting her new manufacturing success. What we Americans did not understand at the time was how to take all these "bits and pieces" and merge them into a finished product. We had a basic understanding of the ingredients, yet we did not have the recipe to bring the ingredients together. While we were unsuccessfully trying to emulate Japanese manufacturing, they became masters of manufacturing and product innovation. Their products not only had higher quality, but they performed better and had more and better features. They also became more expensive, but that didn't dissuade the American consumer who was willing to pay a premium for higher quality. Japan gained as American manufacturing lost market share. Times have grown difficult for American companies. Many began outsourcing component manufacturing to keep product costs down, which frequently resulted in those companies losing even more market share. The death spiral had begun.

What concerns us most are the loss of American jobs and the erosion of American manufacturing expertise and capacity. We are losing the skills that made us the economic power that we once were. Manufacturing and the higher tier professions that were required to support it are vanishing. Engineers, designers, draftsmen, buyers, production control specialists, supervisors, managers, human resource specialists, and others have been laid off in droves. College graduates these days are often without meaningful job opportunities. Instead, they are working in restaurants and other menial service jobs. Students are not selecting manufacturing as a profession because they believe manufacturing in America is dying.

We also face an unprecedented threat to our national defense. Suppose we faced a military challenge and could not ramp up our war machinery like we did in World War II? We could be subservient to the emerging global powers that will have, or already do have, the expertise and capacity to produce the machines of war.

The prevailing myth among many American manufacturers is that we cannot compete with the cheap labor countries. However, our research and experience is that many U.S. companies have developed recipes for success that have made them competitive in a global economy. How do we know this? We (authors Tim Hutzel and Paul Piechota) have a combined 85 years of manufacturing management experience. Our respective organizations, MainStream Management and The Center for Competitive Change at the University of Dayton's Research Institute, have worked with companies that have been successful in competing globally and some that have not. We have learned from the successful companies and have helped the unsuccessful ones achieve higher levels of competitiveness.

Sadly, the new paradigm of American manufacturing is to make it somewhere else. However, not everyone has surrendered to that notion. The authors, Tim Hutzel, president of MainStream Consulting and Paul Piechota, executive director of The Center for Competitive Change at the University of Dayton, have found some examples of manufacturers who have managed to keep most of their work in America.

As the authors have said, "Our purpose in researching these companies is simply to give other American manufacturers a fighting chance to keep their work in America."

Acknowledgments

WE HAD HELP

Besides not really being professional or even novice writers, there was a magnitude of support folks who took time from their schedules to assist, coach, and help us write. The University of Dayton students were especially helpful in taking notes and completing the relentless calls for research and summarizing. It was with their help that we were allowed to listen to the stories and ask question after question in fully understanding each company's success.

Who also helped us, supported our thoughts, and reviewed or edited some of our writings? Below are the contributors we wish to thank for everything they have provided from advice to time and writings. Thank you, team.

- Commissioner Dan Foley, Montgomery County, Dayton, Ohio, opening remarks and enthusiastic support on "retaining work in America"
- Dave Lippert, president, Hamilton Caster, invisible writer, coach, first storyteller
- Joe Patton, CEO of MainStream Management
- Cash Powell, associate director, Center for Competitive Change, second invisible writer, proofreader
- Bill Rieger, graphic artist, marketer, and creator
- Kimberly Pritchard, University of Dayton student, notetaker, researcher, summarizer
- Kate Fahrendorf, University of Dayton student, notetaker, researcher
- Luke Thomas, MainStream Consulting, notetaker, researcher, summarizer
- And, to the authors' wives who just ignored us until they realized we were really writing a book and not just hanging out.

How to Use Our Book

The major difficulty with most how-to or general business books is that the authors leave it up to you to figure out how to use their book. The reader is overwhelmed with page after page of text, diagrams, charts, and information that must be translated into visual images or correlations before you can even begin to understand it. Also, most primers and business books fail because they are so highly overwritten that the general reader becomes hopelessly buried under an avalanche of data—information, scenarios, and facts—which is only vaguely relevant to the reader. Most business readers learn how to execute or run businesses in spite of the textbooks and authors' rhetoric. We will provide the recipes and ingredients used by successful companies that you will understand and implement—just like the Betty Crocker Cookbook®.

There are hundreds of successful companies in the United States that we researched and could have written about. To keep this book simple and practical, we are telling the stories of three companies. They are representative of the many successful companies we found. We will tell the story of how they began and eventually achieved their global competitiveness by creating their own recipes, using simple ingredients.

Our three companies are Hamilton Caster, The Dupps Company, and Midmark. They all have recipes that any company can understand, replicate, or refine. They are all family owned. Each company designs, engineers, and manufactures products that could easily be made offshore. They all have made mistakes and learned along the way.

Each has the highest market share for their product, the highest price, yet the lowest cost. Wouldn't you like to have this, too?

What we researched and uncovered will help you see the recipes and those ingredients on how they got there. We suggest you follow the steps below your first time through the book. Then make it your personal cookbook.

Step No. 1: Read through each company's story, enjoying their history, and learning about the recipes and mixture of ingredients that made them successful in keeping their manufacturing and business in America—successfully and profitably.

Step No. 2: Now, go to our self-assessment to determine what ingredients you have at your company and how well you are using them.

Step No. 3: Go back to the stories and reread the story or section you wish to better understand to build your action plan, such as, calling the company contact or calling the authors, etc.

Step No. 4: Test your plans, try them, review your results, and begin building your own recipes.

Step No. 5: How did your team (direct reports, supervisors, and employees) take to your recipes and ingredients? Did you add, modify, and create your own?

Step No. 6: Share your successes with us by calling or e-mailing on how you kept work in America ... or brought work back.

What They Are Saying about This Book

A book ... a cookbook that brings two pragmatic authors' findings into a simple-to-read book allowing the reader to relate, understand, and duplicate successful American businesses' recipes into their own companies.

The authors debunk the notion American companies have to outsource manufacturing to remain competitive in the global marketplace. The three case studies provide evidence that with the right leadership, companies can increase quality, market share, and profits without shipping jobs overseas. A must read for executives and managers wrestling with outsourcing decisions.

Timothy C. Krehbiel
Professor of Management and
Senior Associate Dean
Farmer School of Business,
Miami University (Ohio)

Keeping Your Business in the U.S.A. finally gives us true insight on why American businesses find it so hard to compete in the global market and inspirational guidance from companies that refuse to believe "Made in USA" is a thing of the past.

Earl Gregorich
Certified Business Advisor,
Ohio SBDC

The book, *Keeping Your Business in the U.S.A.*, is based on the authors' research into how companies are successfully keeping their manufacturing operations in America, and uses three stories plus analytical tools to show the reader by example what and how they are doing. It could become a recipe for American manufacturing companies.

Basil Zabek
*Retired Dayton Development
Coalition and Entrepreneur*

Innovation is what drove manufacturing growth in America in the past and will drive it in the future. This book outlines how a few have used innovation in technology, processes, and/or marketing to be successful.

Harold Linville
*Chief Business Development
Officer/Chairman of the Board*

If there is one thing I've learned in the past 28 years in business, it is that there is no one right answer for improvement. Surviving as a manufacturer in the U.S. is anything but easy. Yet there are clearly some ways to be successful, and this book highlights actual stories of companies making it happen. Odds are, there will be at least a few ideas that resonate in your own business.

Dave Lippert
*President,
Hamilton Caster & Mfg. Co.*

Read it, discuss it, digest it, and live it. The ingredients are here for how you can run a successful business in America.

Bob Lammers
*Marketing Manager (Ret.),
Midmark Corp.*

The backbone of America, our security and financial strength have been borne of our ability as a pioneering people to manufacture and create a strong industrial base for providing innovation coupled with jobs, which in turn drives the flywheel of a strong economic society—without manufacturing in America, we lose our nation's strength, jeopardize our security, weaken overall finances, and quench the hope of strong jobs for our children.

Marc Wolfrum
VP and General Manager,
Cincinnati Sub-Zero Medical Division

Keeping Your Business in the U.S.A. comes at a time when America is searching for how to create and retain jobs.

Joseph Patten
President,
MainStream Management

Section I

Stories of Successful Companies

1

Company Story 1—Small Manufacturer

HAMILTON CASTER

Hamilton Caster is a fourth-generation family manufacturing business started in 1907 by entrepreneur John Weigel in Hamilton, Ohio. John, the son of German immigrants, was determined to be successful in business. His personal drive to succeed, coupled with natural inventiveness fostered a strong beginning. Narrowly surviving the Great Depression, a near-miraculous hand-off to John's daughter preserved the company in family hands into the second generation. Then, led by a very capable son-in-law, the company grew and thrived financially. Ralph Lippert's conservative "pay as you go" philosophy put Hamilton Caster in debt-free condition for his three sons who comprised the third-generation leaders. Bob, Tom, and Larry Lippert applied some unique marketing tactics and prudent investments in facility expansion and modern equipment to further strengthen the company in the material handling market. Currently, the fourth generation faces unparalleled global competition and a moving target in distributor structure as they strive to continue the success. Through it all, four recipes stand out as the main reasons for the company's success:

1. **Conservative financial management and execution**
2. **Consistent leadership in style, process, and management**
3. **Embracing key stakeholders, including employees, customers, vendors, and the union into business strategy**
4. **Employment of new ideas, products, and processes**

Keeping Your B[usiness]

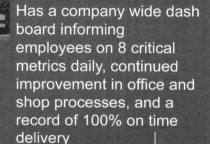

John Weigel is born in Hamilton, Ohio

Has a company wide dash board informing employees on 8 critical metrics daily, continued improvement in office and shop processes, and a record of 100% on time delivery

Hamilton Caster incorporated as [Hamilton] Caster & Mfg. C[o.]

[Hamilto]n Caster wins award from Ohio [Manufa]cturing Association [for effor]ts and results

1907

1[...]

1999

1862

1910

1996

Present

Expan[ds] local to [...]

Weigel forms C.A. Weigel Company selling hardware, sporting goods, and roofing materials. He also buys Stengel caster patents

[...] son of [...] [b]ecomes [presid]ent

Hamilton signs with nationally recognized catalogue house, W.W. Grainger

RECIPE NO. 1

CONSERVATIVE FINANCIAL MANAGEMENT AND EXECUTION

Ingredients

- Cash basis financial system
- Carry little or no debt
- Ensure proper capitalization for the business
- Culture of prudent spending and investing
- Careful planning before spending money

One characteristic that did *not* describe John Weigel was "conservative financial management." While he understood the importance of cash flow, profits, and other core business principles, he could scarcely contain his entrepreneurial enthusiasm to try new things. These flings curtailed the growth of the caster business and, at times, threatened its existence. Fortunately, the strong foundation of casters supported the business through his entrepreneurial meanderings spanning decades.

In 1921, he wanted to produce something for the automotive industry. Unfortunately, John swayed from his core competency, casters. He learned of a tire changer that allowed motorists to change their "Tin Lizzie"[1] tires more easily. He bought the rights to produce the tire changer and then invested in dies, tools, patterns, templates, machinery, and raw materials. However, the tire changer idea was not well thought out. There were too many varieties of automobile wheels at the time, which made the device impractical and sales never materialized.

Further off track from casters, John invested in a spare tire lock, which also fared poorly.

During the years following the start of the Great Depression, even a severe shortage of capital did not keep John from investing in a tangent. He was undeterred by the economic quagmire, ever hopeful for a turnaround. During this time, John bought into another venture outside Hamilton Caster's core competency: automatic coal stokers. The idea seemed sound, as everyone needed to stoke their coal furnaces. He thought the coal stoker was depression proof. Unfortunately, what he did not realize was that the coal stoker was actually a luxury for the very few who could afford it. It was not for the everyday household. The coal stoker quickly became another failed idea.

FAMILY OWNERSHIP CONTINUES

Eventually poor health forced John to retire. The company had very little funds and there were no outside buyers available as the depression worsened. He turned to his daughter, Esther, and her husband, Ralph Lippert, an advertising executive in Cincinnati, to buy the company. With no small risk, the Lipperts bought controlling interest in Hamilton Caster. Ralph could not afford to leave his well-paying advertising position with American Products, Inc., so John continued to serve as president and Ralph helped when and where possible. John's health continued to deteriorate and in 1938, the founder of Hamilton Caster passed away. Esther Lippert succeeded her father as the next president, and one of her first decisions as the president and owner, counseled by her husband, was to drop the coal stoking business. She served as a "bridge" between her father's tenure of leadership and the beginning of her husband's. While not a seasoned veteran in business, she was more than capable of keeping the fledgling company focused on its core competencies and avoiding the flighty fancies that so easily distracted her father.

Several years later, in 1943, Ralph Lippert became the third president of Hamilton Caster. Ralph's legacy during his 33-year presidency was despite his ominous start with no manufacturing experience and only marketing and sales background, and the company successfully posted profits each year of his tenure. As his son, Larry, would later recall, "Dad had good business sense. He always said that the main reason why businesses fail is under-capitalization. He was determined not to let that happen to Hamilton Caster." In some ways, already having a product line of innovative casters and a certain amount of momentum allowed Ralph to focus his sales and marketing experience on broadening the customer base.

CASH BASIS FINANCIAL SYSTEM

The financial legacy continued into the third generation. Bob, Tom, and Larry Lippert, three of Ralph and Esther's four sons, spent most of their working careers at Hamilton Caster. From their earliest days, the principle of fiscal prudence was evident. In 1963, only seven years after joining the firm, Bob negotiated a deal to purchase a local manufacturer and the company paid cash. Towsley Trucks manufactured and sold factory and warehouse trucks, a line that meshed well with Hamilton's existing truck line. When the truck department was at its peak, it took two shifts of factory workers to keep up with demand, and an offsite warehouse to handle the requisite stock for the quick-ship program.

Conservative management enabled the company to avoid layoffs in economic downturns. When one of those downturns ended in 1976, company president Bob Lippert noted as one of his proudest achievements that of "getting through the year without having to lay off a single regular employee." Indeed, Hamilton Caster has operated on a cash basis for most of the years since the Great Depression.

Prudent investment in nearby industrial acreage by the third generation provided a safety net for potential expansion. The plant site in South Hamilton, Ohio, was virtually landlocked by Dixie Highway, the railroad, and properties bordering to the north and south. The purchased industrial lot was eventually sold at a handsome profit, but offered space for a potential move had growth warranted it.

While the land speculation was never put into play, numerous improvements to the manufacturing site increased capacity and improved productivity. Adding a roomier steel bay with overhead crane in the 1960s greatly improved steel-handling capability. The new office building in the 1970s provided much needed breathing space as well as the opportunity to have more modern office equipment. A high-bay warehouse addition in the early 1980s delivered space to store growing inventories of parts and greatly increased handling efficiencies. CNC (computer numerical control) lathes, robot welders, and computerization played significant roles in transformational change in both factory and office. Each improvement was carefully planned, and also carefully planned for in advance. The third generation spent money, but never frivolously or too quickly.

The fourth generation, including Dave, Steve, Jim, and Mark Lippert, has maintained the fiscal conservatism under the watchful eyes of the third generation serving as directors. As recently as 2008, Hamilton Caster was able to purchase a new CNC lathe and pay cash. The serious 2009 recession saw some unfortunate layoffs, but the company scaled back and continued to make money every month.

RECIPE NO. 2

CONSISTENT LEADERSHIP IN STYLE, PROCESS, AND MANAGEMENT

Ingredients

- Leaders selected from family members
- Family members working at the company during their school years
- Family members must first hold professional positions outside the company
- Finding positions within the company to fit the style and talent of the leaders
- Treat employees like they are family and with respect
- Active leadership in creating a cultural shift of Lean[2]
- Everyone accountable via process and products metrics

Hamilton Caster has been blessed with only five presidents in its 103-year history. Considering that the second president, Esther Lippert (daughter of founder John Weigel), served in that role for only four years, the tenures of the remaining four have been significant. A clear advantage of this is the consistency for the employees as well as the tendency to "stay the course" and avoid quick changes that characterize many companies.

FIRST GENERATION: ENTREPRENEURIAL PIONEERING

John Weigel, son of German immigrants, was destined to become Hamilton Caster's first president. Getting there was much more than a simple walk in the park, though. John's father had come to Hamilton in 1850 to find new world opportunities unavailable in Germany. The son learned quickly from his father that hard work bore rewards of achievement, satisfaction, and wealth.

Since he liked to tinker with his hands, John initially thought he would become a machinist. He began as a machinist's apprentice for a local business, but soon realized that he didn't like the drudgery of a machinist's life. His dream was bigger than that—to someday own his own company.

Leaving the machinist job, he found a new position as a freight claims agent with the Cincinnati, Hamilton, and Dayton Railroad Company. This job offered him a good income to support his growing family of seven children. It provided financial stability for his family, but did nothing to satisfy his inner entrepreneurial cravings. He still worked for others and continued to dream about the day he could be his own boss.

In his spare time, John tinkered in his garage, applying his machining skills to create a product that he could take to market. Oddly enough, casters fascinated him and he worked on several of his own ideas. His inventiveness was beginning to show.

The plan to own a business started to take shape in 1907. A friend of his, Charles Stengel, decided to start a business to manufacture a new style caster he had invented for his family's furniture company. Stengel's caster design was for double-wheeled units that used tough roller bearings and antifriction swiveling action to assure smooth operation. He discovered how to make them so they did not lock up after rigorous use or cause excessive wear on carpets and flooring.

Aware of John's interest in casters and background in machining, Charles Stengel asked him to join the new company. John couldn't quit his secure railroad job, but he did accept the offer on a part-time basis. Although the company had some initial successes, Charles Stengel's poor business skills and his under-estimation of business start-up costs resulted in failure. While John was now out a part-time job, he had learned some valuable lessons that would help him in the near future.

Later in 1907, with several of his family members, he formed the C. A. Weigel Company. The new family-owned company sold hardware, sporting goods, and roofing materials to the general public in Hamilton, Ohio. After three years of success, John renamed the business the Hamilton Caster and Mfg. Company, bought the idle Stengel caster patents, and began production of the casters originally designed by Charles Stengel.

To say that John's company had early difficulties would be an understatement. He was still carrying two jobs. Cash flow was tight and most of the sales revenues went directly back into the company to invest in equipment and new caster innovations. He was determined not to suffer the same fate as his friend, Charles Stengel.

John knew that to stay in business new products had to be continually introduced and current product lines expanded. John learned of the need for a much heavier-duty caster. To meet this need, the company designed and began producing a heavy-duty, double-wheeled caster that became popular in the New England shoe industry. Sales increased and the company continued to grow.

Soon sales stretched from regional to national, and John designed and built even heavier-duty casters, which added to his growing customer base. In 1927, he recognized an opportunity to diversify his offerings in the material handling business, and he purchased the Zering Company. Zering was a local Cincinnati manufacturer of nonpowered factory trucks and carts. John wisely purchased only the rights and equipment to make the products, and added floor space and capacity to his existing factory in Hamilton. During the booming 1920s, this purchase was a stroke of genius as Hamilton Casters was able to take better advantage of a growing market.

October 23, 1929: The official start of the Great Depression. Sales at Hamilton Caster declined to less than 20 percent of their peak in the first three quarters of the year. Still, John and his company soldiered on. He was forced to borrow significantly in the late 1930s, and reduced his workforce (which he considered family) from 35 to 11. And, those 11 were only working part time. Business conditions improved ever so gradually, but tragedy struck John in the form of two strokes, which he suffered in 1936. At 74 years of age, his body was telling him it was time to slow down.

He attempted to sell his company, but received no serious offers until his own daughter, Esther, and son-in-law agreed to purchase Hamilton Caster. Son-in-law Ralph Lippert was an advertising manager for American Products Company in Cincinnati. The purchase agreement left John in the role of president, as Ralph determined to remain at his advertising job until he could learn more about the caster business. Esther Lippert was to control the board and oversee corporate finances. In this role, she could prevent any ill-advised forays into unknown markets that had characterized John's tenure.

The new arrangement was short-lived, as John Weigel passed away from a stroke in July 1938. Esther succeeded her father as president while Ralph continued in his job in Cincinnati. However, he had a significant "behind the scenes" role in the company. Esther's passion for the business and its employees garnered her support and admiration during a time both were needed. Her leadership helped Hamilton Caster survive into the World War II years.

SECOND GENERATION: MANAGEMENT AND MARKETING

By 1943, Ralph Lippert decided to make his career switch and assumed the leadership of Hamilton Caster as its third president. He had survived the Great Depression and built into the company's DNA an aversion to debt. He was not opposed to risk, however. Buying a struggling manufacturing company during the Depression while raising a family of four boys and with a mortgage on a new home was definitely a risk. But, as late as the 1970s, he was opposed to the purchase of property adjacent to the company's plant site in Hamilton. He left that risk to his three sons who had joined him by that time. Essentially, they had to buy it on their own.

Ralph's legacy included the company making a profit every one of his 33 years as president. The Depression years had taught him fiscal prudence. He also promoted the business through aggressive advertising, his forte. Yet, even with his diligence, attention to every detail of the business, and penchant for hard work, he attributed much of the company's success to the war years and resulting increased business.

Ralph's oldest son, Bob, joined the company in 1956. By that time, he had considerable experience working in the plant most summers of his youth. After a brief stint in the army in New Jersey, he realized his personal dream of working at Hamilton Caster. His mechanical engineering degree from the University of Cincinnati would serve him well in his leadership of a manufacturing company.

One year later, in 1957, Bob's younger brother, Tom, joined him at Hamilton Caster. Tom held a master's degree in English from the University of North Carolina, and he had completed a tour of duty in the navy. Tom's passion lay in marketing and sales, a perfect complement to his older brother. His idea for Pronto[3] service would later transform the company into an industry-leading, quick-ship manufacturer.

Younger brother Larry spent time in other pursuits before joining Hamilton Caster in 1968. Larry had a master's degree in English from Loyola University in Chicago, and had worked as a teacher and sold textbooks. Larry settled into sales, a role that fit both his outgoing personality and his previous experience.

One interesting side note to the fact that three of the four sons of Ralph and Esther spent all or most of their working careers at Hamilton Caster is that none were particularly encouraged to join the company and work with their father. While it might have seemed to be destiny in the case of Bob, there was never an expectation that any would consider the small manufacturing company the place of their life's work.

THIRD GENERATION: GROWTH AND MODERNIZATION

The third generation inspired and promoted the purchase of Towsley Trucks in 1963. Similar to Zering, Towsley was a local manufacturer of factory material handling equipment. Bob Lippert saw an opportunity to broaden Hamilton's product line with a separate Towsley line of equipment. When the deal was consummated, Hamilton Caster owned the Towsley line, marketing it as Towsley Trucks, and was able to pay cash for the purchase. Bob's father may not have led the charge, but he insisted on applying financial wisdom to it.

Other changes followed the Towsley purchase. A sizable addition, including a large overhead crane in a new steel bay, graced the south end of the truck plant in 1966. Demand for more products led to the creation of a second shift in the factory. Tom's idea for Pronto (quick ship) service helped the Hamilton's many distributors sell product without having to stock.

The third generation also continued the development of new products at the heavy-duty end of the market, including the introduction of forged steel casters and wheels. A long-running marketing campaign aimed at the many distributors, called "Hamilton Heroes," recognized the loyal distributors and resulted in increased sales.

Ralph Lippert retired 1976, and son Bob was named Hamilton Caster's fourth president. Sadly, the elder Lippert passed away just a few months later before he could enjoy much of a well-deserved retirement. By this time, with many years of overlap, the third generation had learned key business lessons from the second generation and was also applying many of their own ideas. This transition was seamless, at least from outside the company.

Bob's leadership style was summed up as: "Conservative, honest, nice to do business with. A quality image." Indeed, Bob quickly earned the respect of everyone who knew him. He was a people person.

Modernization of the business and the product line accelerated under the third generation. They oversaw the computerization of the business, expansion of the product line, addition of new technologies in manufacturing, and renewed focus on meeting customers' needs for special products. This resulted in an era of increased sales and profits for Hamilton Caster.

In 1982, the first of the fourth generation of family began working full time at Hamilton Caster. Dave Lippert, fresh from six years of air force duty, joined the company. As was true of the previous generation, there were no expectations by Bob or his brothers that their offspring would or should work with them at Hamilton Caster. Each of the fourth generation made his/her own career decision.

Three years later, after a couple of tours in the army, Bob's second son, Steve, joined the company. His background in both marketing and human resources equipped him well for making a strong contribution. Younger brother Jim followed in 1990, also after some time in the army. Like his Uncle Larry, Jim was a natural for the inside sales work. Tom's younger son, Mark, decided to leave the West Coast and begin a career at Hamilton Caster in 1995. His interest in marketing may have been inherited from his father, but he added the critical element of information technology (IT). To date, this completes the fourth generation family management.

Again, a significant period of overlap prepared the fourth generation for leadership. Tom retired in 1991, and mentored Steve in his roles of marketing and serving as the company treasurer. Larry followed by retiring in 1993, leaving sufficient time to groom Jim as the next sales manager. Bob retired a year later, and the board named Dave as the company's fifth president. By that date, Dave had worked with his father for 12 years. Bob served as the company president for 18 of his 38-year career.

The fourth generation ran headlong into a world of ferocious import competition, proving the title of Thomas Friedman's book *The World is Flat* (Picador, 2005). Some moves were obvious. Mark created a first-class Web site and promptly put Hamilton Caster at the front of the pack. Steve suggested tightening the parameters of Pronto by shipping even faster, and then proposed adding many more items to the Pronto "mix." The plant temporarily hiccupped, but soon adapted to the new challenge. New business software proved painful initially, but eventually became a major tool for improving corporate performance.

Perhaps the most significant contribution to date is the beginning of a Lean journey. It is too early to tell, but the fourth generation legacy may be this Lean journey and the accompanying cultural change. A major part of this is engaging everyone in the company to propose and implement improvements to the business.

After an initial surge in 1996, which was followed by almost 10 years of stagnation and regression, the company leaders regrouped and set a course for continuous improvement and universal involvement. Office processes, as well as factory operations, have been overhauled along the way. Metrics support the changes, and also point out the need for additional changes. Annual "hoshin[4] planning" sets the course for the entire company, and established annual improvement goals contributing to significant long-term improvements. The fourth generation has discovered the power of many and is engaging it daily to improve the business.

Spanning 102 years, the leadership at Hamilton Caster met the needs of the time. John Weigel, founder and first-generation president, led as an entrepreneur. He was creative and needed raw courage to launch a company. The need for business sophistication would come later. John started the Hamilton Caster flywheel spinning.

Esther and Ralph Lippert followed her father and brought marketing strength and business acumen to the company. They also provided more corporate structure, which helped guide the company's growth as the company emerged from the Great Depression. The flywheel was spinning faster.

The third generation, consisting of the three brothers, provided a major shot of innovation in both products and sales, notably the Pronto system. During this period, the company enjoyed significant growth. This was also a period of modernization in facilities and equipment, adding much to the productivity.

FOURTH GENERATION: BATTLING GLOBAL COMPETITION

Intense global competition met the fourth generation as it began to lead. Continuing to run the business in the same fashion was not a viable option. The current leadership initiated a Lean journey of continuous improvement and total employee engagement. Performance measurements flourished and, coupled with goals and frequent reviews, propelled the company into major gains in virtually every area.

Although each generation faced different challenges and responded in unique ways, some common themes define the family management at Hamilton Caster. Common family values, including integrity and a degree of paternalism, characterize the leadership.

Tenure, or staying power, provided stability. Each generation was engaged for decades, avoiding the problems of frequent leadership changes and the challenges that employees can face trying to learn and adapt to new management styles and focuses.

Additionally, there was adequate time for each succeeding generation to learn from the previous one. Therefore, transitions were smooth for all stakeholders, including employees, customers, and vendors.

Finally, the commitment to family members is evident as new leaders have been groomed from within the business. This makes it likely that this business will continue into the future as a family business. Even the family members not employed at the company are stakeholders through corporate ownership and have strong interest in the company's success. Hamilton Caster's legacy is imprinted on each member and is one more thing that unites this family.

RECIPE NO. 3

**EMBRACING KEY STAKEHOLDERS INCLUDING
EMPLOYEES, CUSTOMERS, VENDOR, AND
THE UNION INTO BUSINESS STRATEGY**

Ingredients

- Create a culture of total employee involvement
- Treat employees and the union like they are family and with respect
- Create a culture of trust

From its inception, Hamilton Caster has been a family business. The founder, John Weigel, saw to that on Day One. After seeing Charles Stengel's startup company fail soon after Weigel had joined it part time, he knew firsthand the pitfalls and fragility of a new business. He also had a fresh surge of entrepreneurship in his veins.

John was so determined to own his own company that later in 1907, with several of his family members, he formed the C. A. Weigel Company. The family-owned company sold hardware, sporting goods, and roofing materials to the general public in Hamilton, Ohio. After three years of success, he renamed the business the Hamilton Caster and Mfg. Company, bought the Stengel caster patents, and began production of the casters designed by Charles Stengel.

John's children inherited their father's love of business and hard work and some began working in the family business. John's son, Herb, worked for the company for 55 years, longer than any other employee or family member. Herb joined the board of the company in the early 1920s when John's brother-in-law, Tony Krogman, passed away. Tony had served as vice president of the board. About that same time, John hired Max Conrad, his first cousin, as corporate secretary. He knew Max's qualities, and depended on him to provide John more time for product development and business expansion.

John's undying loyalty to employees was perhaps best demonstrated in his handling of George Kalberer, a top machinist. Unfortunately, George was also a part-time counterfeiter, a crime that landed him in prison. After his prison stint, George returned to John to apologize and ask for a job. John accepted his apology and rehired him. The two actually developed a new caster and received a U.S. patent on the design.

His daughter, Esther, worked as a stenographer and lived at home until her marriage to Ralph Lippert in 1926. In time, she would own a large share of the company, also serving as president from 1939 to 1942. Her husband Ralph would be president from 1943 to 1976.

Ralph Lippert became president in 1943 when he began working at Hamilton Caster full time. Manufacturing was new to him and even though he was president, he was also the new kid on the block. Ralph had to learn the business from the ground up and quickly. He brought a strong background and knowledge in advertising and marketing and began to advertise and market Hamilton Caster's products and a reputation to bring new and increased sales and brand recognition.

Ralph also brought new sales ideas to the company. He relied on long-term relationships that were nurtured with customers and industrial distributors. His legacy during his 33-year presidency was despite his ominous start with no manufacturing experience and only marketing and sales background, the company successfully posted profits each year of his tenure.

Ralph and Esther's family was also growing. They had three sons who eventually joined the business: Bob, Tom, and Larry. In 1956, Bob Lippert, a mechanical engineering graduate from the University of Cincinnati, was the first of the three brothers to actually begin working for the firm full time. Tom, Bob's younger brother, was next to join Hamilton Caster. In 1957, while Bob concentrated his interests and efforts in manufacturing, Tom dived into sales and marketing. He wanted to meet more often with contacts in person, and even if this was not the way of his predecessors, it was tried and met with much success. In 1968, the team expanded as Larry, Bob and Tom's younger brother, joined the company as the internal sales manager.

The transition to the fourth generation began in the early 1990s. The company saw the third generation of the family retire, first Larry, then Tom and Bob.

In 1995 Dave Lippert, Bob's oldest son, became the next president succeeding his father. Steve, Dave's brother, assumed multiple roles as executive vice president and manager of human resources, finance, and marketing. Dave's other brother, Jim, assumed the role of internal sales manager and Tom's son, Mark, became the vice president of marketing. The fourth generation of the Lippert family was clearly in charge and ready to put their mark on the business world and next growth for Hamilton Caster.

ENGAGING EMPLOYEES, UNION, SUPPLIERS, CUSTOMERS

The fourth generation began to face challenges the previous generations never even imagined, particularly offshore competition. Imports from Mexico, Taiwan, India, China, Malaysia, and other low-labor cost countries started competing with Hamilton Caster. Price to the customer became the major issue. Hamilton Caster's top line and bottom line became very vulnerable.

In 1992, Marc Wolfrum, son of long-term employee Hermann Wolfrum, joined the company as manufacturing manager and brought with him experiences from his recent past employer General Electric, i.e., notably, production cells. What happened next set the stage for the company's survival and growth.

Engaging employees for their ideas on improving the business, really listening to them, and then implementing many of those ideas became the new theme. It began in 1996 with the formation of the first production cell. Against a strong traditional paradigm, a cross-functional team adopted "one piece flow" in the production of a major portion of the product line. Shop and office people working side-by-side to accomplish a goal resulted in a brand new chemistry in the company. Every employee gained influence and each one became more of a stakeholder.

Hamilton Caster's next large change was to break down physical and departmental walls and bring everyone together to work as a team; actually, two teams: one for casters, Team Caster, and another team for trucks, Team Trucks. Employees worked together like never before in company history to move furniture, remove walls, and construct an environment where communication is enhanced, productivity is improved, and everyone feels a tighter bond to the work.

TREATING EVERYONE LIKE FAMILY

Hamilton Caster is a family business. Family has been employed, served on the board, and benefitted as shareholders. Employees in large measure have been treated as family. Many work at the company their entire careers and choose to retire from Hamilton Caster. Connections span generations. For example, the most senior factory employee (a welder in the truck department) recalls his being hired by Ralph Lippert, the company's third president and member of the second generation.

One of the anticipated hurdles faced by the fourth generation has been the unionized shop workers. But, in this case, any barrier has been remediated and new, higher levels of trust in both directions ensure positive results. Hourly workers happily join improvement teams to work on week-long projects. Salaried workers engage in shop projects and get dirty as they help to move equipment and clean up areas of the factory.

Recognizing customers and embracing them as stakeholders is another new facet of Hamilton's Lean journey. Early in the journey at least one major distributor visited the original production cell and was so impressed they sent a congratulatory plaque honoring what they had seen. The value for customers was a more dependable flow of product.

Business connections with constituents such as the company's accounting firm date back three generations. Some key vendors have supplied parts and services for decades. The most recent development, the Lean journey begun in earnest in 2007, engages everyone in and out of the company in deliberate and developmental ways. Employees are entrusted with new levels of responsibilities, asked to provide and implement ideas for improvement, and involved in teams to solve problems and improve every facet of the business. Teams are cross functional, and shop employees interact with office employees as members of improvement teams. There is a new, higher level of trust and communication throughout the company. Success is shared and promoted, and contributors are recognized for their roles. The culture is changing to fit the times and the challenges.

> **RECIPE NO. 4**
>
> **EMPLOYMENT OF NEW IDEAS, PRODUCTS, AND SERVICES**
>
> **Ingredients**
>
> - Broaden product line that complements existing expertise and diversify
> - Shorten lead times to customers
> - Lean transformation to ensure all processes are under constant improvement
> - Treat customers like they are royalty
> - Vendor evaluation and improvement program
> - Hoshin Kanri[4] as the means to involve the entire company in Lean

John Weigel was an entrepreneur. His dream and passion was to make something, and to be his own boss. It took some time and more than a few dead ends before he settled on casters. Despite a number of diversions and distractions along the way, the business of casters has always been the foundation of Hamilton Caster.

John knew that to stay in business new products had to be continually introduced and current product lines expanded. The company designed and began producing a heavy-duty, double-wheeled caster that caught on in the New England shoe industry. Sales increased and the company continued to grow.

PRODUCT QUALITY AND DURABILITY

Hamilton Caster began to develop a reputation for "built-to-last" and "high-quality" products. Special orders and customization further defined its niche. Customers felt they had an engineering firm working specifically on their problem when they purchased products from Hamilton Caster. The company's willingness to adapt products set Hamilton Caster apart; it would become an important part of the firm's future.

John Weigel continued to design and manufacture high-capacity casters that could carry considerably more load. He remained focused on his product lines and how to broaden or deepen their uses and marketability.

In 1927, he found a new opportunity. It came in the form of the Zering Manufacturing Co., a firm in nearby Cincinnati. Zering made nonpowered factory trucks and casters. When John learned the company was up for sale, he knew he wanted to buy it. After all, it was in a similar business.

He bought only the rights and equipment to produce the trucks and casters, not its land and buildings. Acquiring Zering doubled Hamilton Caster's size, placed it into a growing market, and set the stage for the future. Now boosted by the resources of Zering, Hamilton Caster could afford to reinvent itself as a broader material-handling company: casters and hand trucks.

The combination of casters and nonpowered platform trucks continues today to be the mainstay of Hamilton Caster's product line.

ADVANCING PRODUCTS THROUGH MARKETING

The 1940s brought Ralph Lippert to Hamilton Caster full time and as its third president (following the four-year presidency of his wife, Esther, John Weigel's daughter). Manufacturing was new to him and even though he was president, he was also the new kid on the block. Ralph brought a strong background and knowledge in advertising and marketing and began to advertise and market Hamilton Caster's products and reputation to bring new and increased sales and brand recognition.

Ralph introduced many new products that added to the growing list of customers. Hamilton Caster focused on being the provider of long-lasting and high-quality products that could be customized if the customer desired. Ralph also brought new sales ideas to the company. He relied on long-term relationships that were nurtured with customers and industrial distributors.

THE CUSTOMER IS KING

The company's philosophy was to do anything its customers required. It was once said that "we want our customers to think we are a bigger company than we actually are." Hamilton Caster's credo was to over-deliver on performance and service. This was a family business built on specialization and customer satisfaction. The company was growing at a substantial pace.

The third generation began arriving in the 1950s. Ralph Lippert's sons, Bob and Tom, began working as a great team. Their goal was to modernize and expand the company while their father continued to guide them from the president's chair. In 1963, the company bought Towsley Trucks, a local competitor who made a variety of hand trucks. This purchase was like a modern-day Zering opportunity. The acquisition strengthened Hamilton Caster's position in the region and elevated them into the national hand truck market sector. In 1968, the team expanded as Larry Lippert, Bob and Tom's brother, joined the company as the sales manager.

The new team expanded the facilities. They installed and upgraded computer systems and trained all the employees to use them, both in the office and in the factory.

PRODUCT DEVELOPMENT AND INTRODUCTION

Several new products were introduced during this time period. The success of these new product introductions by the market validated the company's ability to engineer and build superior and durable casters. The so-called miracle wheel, named Duralast, with urethane tread was tested out by Ohio's snow plows and showed no signs of wear while competitors' standard rubber casters quickly failed. This story produced great advertising to prospective customers.

This new success and positive positioning against their competition didn't find the Lippert family sitting on their laurels. A new promotion tool was invented by Tom, quick ship Pronto. Pronto committed Hamilton Caster to ship most catalog orders within 48 hours. Tom's idea revolutionized the industry and sent competitors scrambling to fulfill orders faster. The premise of Pronto was that Hamilton Casters would ship orders from its distributors to the end users quickly and at no additional charge. Distributors would not be required to stock Hamilton products, but could still promise quick delivery to their customers. To the distributors, there wouldn't be the expense of stocking a plethora of parts (not knowing exactly which combinations their customers might need) and they would not have to handle the parts internally.

The third-generation team continued to improve and modernize the business. They added computer numerically controlled machines in the shop along with new robotic welders. They also continued developing and introducing new products including the forged steel casters. Computerizing the shop helped significantly with scheduling systems, and CNC machine tools and robots helped maintain some level of market advantage.

The transition to the fourth generation began in the early 1990s. The company saw the third generation of family retire, first Tom, then Larry and Bob. Dave, Steve, Jim, and, eventually Mark, joined the firm as the fourth generation of family leaders.

Some of the fourth-generation changes have built on past successes. The number of stock-keeping units (SKUs) available for the celebrated Pronto quick ship program continued to grow significantly. Some of industry's heaviest-rated casters became Pronto. Also, the bar was raised even higher as the pledged shipping time shrank to same day in some cases. Orders placed for Pronto items in the morning were shipping that afternoon. The rest shipped the next business day. The balance of the company's (non-Pronto) orders saw accelerated deliveries as the company shrank lead times to gain competitive advantage.

The fourth-generation Lipperts had not been exposed to production cells,[5] but, because of their faith in plant manager Marc Wolfrum, in 1996, they launched a six-month project to create a production cell in one of their top-selling product lines. The effort was so successful that not only did they achieve the same business results that Marc experienced at GE, but Hamilton Caster won the annual award from the Ohio Manufacturing Association for their efforts and results, a competition of more than 200 companies. Production cells and office improvements continued to be implemented throughout the company.

The next major hurdle was to work on the top line, sales, and revamp the Web-based online ordering system. Mark Lippert applied his knowledge of company products with marketing technique and IT skills to create what is recognized as an industry leader. Hamilton Caster's Web-based system makes it easy for catalog shoppers, a large part of their market, to do business with the company.

LEAN AS A STRATEGY AND A TACTIC

The Lean journey, initiated in 1995 with award-winning success, but then left to languish for almost 10 years, reemerged in 2007 with the engagement of MainStream Management for guidance and the hiring of a full-time Lean leader for commitment. Hoshin planning became the driving force for sustained and targeted change. Hoshin Kanri, also known as *policy deployment* in western management, helps the organization look three to five years in the future to develop breakthrough objectives that will fundamentally change the way the organization behaves. It also aligns organizational resources to achieve shorter goals supporting the three- to five-year goals. Hoshin Kanri was the glue needed to get everyone moving in the same direction. In 2007, Hamilton Caster began its Hoshin Kanri journey. Now, instead of a few management personnel conducting blitz kaizens[6] here and there with bright, but fading results, the entire company, from top to bottom, is engaged in an organized, company-wide game plan moving Hamilton Caster forward into the future.

For a small family-led manufacturing business, this change in style and culture was transformational. Leadership was not simply listening to employees, rather, it was asking them to become more involved, and giving them authority to make significant changes to carry out their own improvement ideas. A new style of leadership is emerging as the fourth generation builds its legacy.

The journey has engaged stakeholders outside the company as well. A vendor evaluation project saw the top 10 vendors invited in for visits and plant tours emphasizing the importance of the products provided to the company's delivery to its customers. A quarterly evaluation scoring was unveiled, with explanation of the scoring elements and criteria. Interestingly, all 10 vendors were very much in favor of the new process and looked forward to working in a measured environment.

More than any point in the company's past, the fourth generation is promoting more and more goals and measurements, corrective action based on gaps between goals and performance, and involvement in decision making and goal setting by virtually everyone.

Hamilton Caster's history is sprinkled with an almost continuous development of new and more robust products, increasing emphasis on meeting customers' special needs with custom-engineered products, adaptation to changing markets and technologies by aggressively working to be the best at all times in marketing and advertising, and an evolution of management style that embraces the best skills, abilities, and ideas of all the employees.

END NOTES

1. Tin Lizzie: Nickname for the 1908 Ford Model T automobile.
2. Lean: A form of continuous process improvement whereby the elimination of waste is the primary goal; often associated with the Toyota Production System.
3. Pronto: A registered trademark of Hamilton Caster and Mfg. Co. to designate products that are guaranteed to ship within 48 hours of being ordered.
4. Hoshin Kanri: A method of policy deployment and strategic decision making that focuses and aligns the organization on a few vital "breakthrough" improvements. The objectives and means to achieve the objectives are cascaded down through the entire organization using a series of linked matrices. The process is self-correcting and encourages organizational learning and continuous improvement of the planning process itself.
5. Production Cells: An alignment of processes and equipment in correct process sequence, where operators work within the cell and materials are presented to them from the outside of the cell.
6. Kaizens: Japanese for *change for the better* or *improvement*. A business philosophy of continuous cost reduction, reducing quality problems, and delivery time reduction through rapid, team-based improvement activity.

2

Company Story 2—Medium Manufacturer

THE DUPPS COMPANY

The Dupps Company is a fourth-generation, family business that designs, manufactures, installs, and services rendering equipment. What is rendering? It is the process of converting inedible animal parts into proteins and oils for the animal feed and cosmetic industries. The Dupps Company (Germantown, Ohio) has always been clearly focused on its niche in the rendering industry. From its beginning, The Dupps Company decided to offer the most dependable, efficient, and well-serviced equipment in its industry. This decision has garnered them the enviable position of best in class with the highest market share.

The Dupps Company has employed three core recipes to garner such long-term success. Quite simple in statements, the execution of each reaches back four generations and depends on laser-like focus. They include:

1. **Market clarity**
2. **Employment of ideas, products, and services**
3. **Family leadership and management**

Keeping Your B[usiness]

John J. Dupps joins
Cincinnati Butcher Supply

J[
G[

[D]UKE is
[bo]ught out by
[th]e Dupps
[Co]mpany

DUKE
Construction is
bought by The
Dupps Company

John Jr. leaves
Germantown R[
with friend, Ma[

1886   1935   1972   1972

───

1930   1977   2010

John Jr. fo[
Dupps Co[
JAK as its

Dave Dupps starts
at company

John J. Dupps, Jr.
follows his father in
working for CBS

[Hank] Jr.
[   ]president

Frank Dupps Jr., son of
Hank Dupps, becomes
the new President of The
Dupps Company

[utzel] & Paul Piechota

50 miles north of Cincinnati. The ferret farm raised ferrets for their pelts, but needed to dispose of the carcasses. John Jr. visited the ferret farm and explained to the owners that rendering the carcasses would not only dispose of the carcasses, but it also would provide another revenue stream by enabling the farm to sell the oil and meal from the rendering process. John Jr. was successful in selling the rendering equipment to the ferret farm.

Not long after that, John Jr. left The Cincinnati Butcher's Supply Company. He and his friend, Robert McTavish (Mac, as he was known), partnered to form a new company: the Germantown Rendering Company. John Jr., however, was more interested in manufacturing than running the rendering company, and he sold his share of the Germantown Rendering Company to Mac, who remained in Germantown to run the rendering business and sell tallow and other rendered products. John Jr. was now free to begin his manufacturing operation as a new company, which he did in 1935, naming it the John J. Dupps Company. He scarcely had opportunity to launch the new business when he unexpectedly passed away at the age of 40. His son, Jack, took over the company at a tender and inexperienced age of 25.

Jack, with some help from Mac in Germantown, made contact with a Frank Schottelkotte. Jack and Frank traveled the country looking for opportunities to sell their products. Jack traveled more than 150 days a year, sometimes in stretches as long as three weeks. He disliked sales work, but knew that for his business to succeed, it was necessary. For Jack, it was a serious lesson in learning customer needs as well as indoctrination into the rendering market.

PRODUCT BREAKTHROUGH

During his travels, Jack met Jack Keith, an engineer from Los Angeles. At this time, rendering was a very labor-intensive, batch processing system. First, raw material from slaughterhouses was cooked. It was then emptied into presses that squeezed the fat out of the protein. Jack Keith believed a new continuous process could replace the traditional batch filling and emptying, which was standard in the rendering industry. He believed the new continuous rendering would revolutionize the industry.

In the late 1950s, Jack Dupps and Jack Keith designed the first version of the continuous rendering process and began marketing and selling the new system. Having the vision to foresee continuous rendering could become the gold standard for rendering, they patented the process and equipment. Jack Dupps now had two rendering products that needed his full attention: batch rendering, which continued to be sold by The Dupps Company, and continuous rendering, which would be sold through a newly formed company, DUKE, Inc. During the transition time between batch and continuous rendering, there was a need for marketing and selling both types of systems. Coincidentally, Mac became available when the Germantown Rendering Company was closed. He knew many people in the rendering business and knew the business inside and out, but only the batch system. Frank Schottelkotte became the continuous system sales specialist and Mac concentrated on batch applications.

SUFFERING THROUGH THE GROWING PAINS

The first DUKE continuous rendering systems sold had plenty of bugs to be worked out. The system was sold to Denver Rendering Co., and it had some major unsolved issues when put in operation. Meanwhile, DUKE was installing another system in New York for The Van Iderstein Co. The pressure on Jack Dupps and Jack Keith was intense. If they didn't make things right for these customers, they would not get paid and their reputation would be irreparably damaged. Not only that, but they would not learn what needed to be corrected for future systems. Through sheer determination and faith in the continuous rendering system, they were able to make the systems work. With the crises behind them, they could concentrate again on building the business.

Years passed and the next generation of the Dupps family gained experience in the family business. Eventually, two of Jack Dupps' sons were ready to join full time: John Avery, Jr. (John) and Frank (Hank).

NECESSITY IS THE MOTHER OF INVENTION AND OPPORTUNITY

In the 1970s, the rendering market was growing. Meat and poultry processing companies and rendering companies were developing plans to construct totally new rendering systems from the ground up. This would require buying the rendering systems and engineering the buildings to house the systems. Senior management for the food processing and rendering companies were inundated by the sheer volume of orders they received and the decisions they had to make on which vendors to choose. Bids had to be sent out for architects to design the building, general contractors to build the facility, rendering suppliers to engineer the rendering system, and specialists to handle environmental compliance, building code compliance, zoning regulations, etc.

Dupps saw this as an opportunity to offer one-stop shopping to the managers and owners who would now need only one point of contact. Dupps would take care of designing and building the entire operation, called a turnkey system. Customers loved the concept. These turnkey[2] systems were predominantly continuous rendering systems, so Dupps used the DUKE brand name and formed a new company, DUKE Construction.

DUKE Construction, with its turnkey system, was very popular during the boom years of the rendering market, but as people's eating habits shifted toward nonmeat products, fewer new facilities were in demand and DUKE Construction was disbanded when Frank Schottelkotte retired in the late 1980s.

Jack Dupps' youngest son, Dave, was now ready to join the company. In 1991, Hank's son, Frank, joined the company and shortly thereafter, Hank's other son, Matt, also began his career with The Dupps Company. The fourth generation was now in place.

Frank worked in sales and business development. He conceived the idea of getting into the fish rendering market, a new arena for Dupps. Frank did his homework on this idea. He shared his findings at the annual company business planning meeting and was tasked to pursue the idea. He spent a day in Norway with a fish company consultant who said there were no barriers to entry for Dupps. The company is now pursuing that market because of Frank's initiative. He also spends considerable time in Latin America working with companies to introduce Dupps technology.

GROWTH THROUGH INNOVATION

Finding new markets and new products is a never-ending necessity for any company, especially for The Dupps Company. The U.S. rendering market has become flat, if not declining, in recent years due to consolidation of customers and lower exports of meat products. Frank's contribution of uncovering new markets in Latin America is only part of the total effort. Dupps has exported its products and technology worldwide for over 50 years. As export market conditions have changed, Dupps has learned how to adapt its distribution channels to continue to serve its international customers.

Marketing by "being involved with customers" has taught Dupps that by staying connected with its customers it can learn the customers' needs and problems. When a Dupps service representative is at a customer's facility, he has the opportunity to discuss current and future needs. This communication has led to new products and services, such as the Machine Inspection Program. This program is a series of scheduled inspections that typically lead to preventive repairs or replacements for the customer's rendering system components. It's a practical way of staying in touch with the customer and gathering sales intelligence while providing value added services.

Adapting existing products to new applications has also been a way for The Dupps Company to expand into different markets. For example, the Dupps Pressor®, a component of a rendering system that continuously squeezes out fats from rendered solids, was successfully modified for use in the oilseed processing industry.

Today, the Dupps Company dominates the rendering market with an 85-percent market share in the United States and a 60-percent market share in Europe. Dupps' market share is driven by relationships, performance, durability, and service.

The company works very hard to know each customer on a personal and professional basis. Dupps uses personal visits, conventions, trade shows, and other events to meet and talk with customers. Dupps builds personal relationships with its customers so they feel comfortable sharing their needs and desires. The Dupps Company wants to understand its customers' exact needs and expectations.

Dupps is both inward and outward looking. The company is conscious about the viability of its core business: designing, building, and installing heavy-duty process equipment. Theirs is a small niche market that, if either saturated or penetrated by competitors, could have serious negative consequences. One way Dupps safeguards this is to look from within during its Annual Business Planning Meeting. This meeting, attended by upper- and middle-level managers, focuses on those things that went well, not so well, and what might be done going forward.

> **RECIPE NO. 2**
>
> **EMPLOYMENT OF IDEAS, PRODUCTS, AND SERVICES**
> **Ingredients**
> - Taking advantage of at-hand opportunities
> - Culture of not letting people down
> - Applying trial and error in developing new products and services
> - Product development and continuous improvement are ongoing activities
> - Products many times more robust and effective than the competition
> - Unparalleled customer service

When John J. Dupps, Jr. joined the Cincinnati Butcher's Supply Company, the idea seed of rendering was officially planted. Perhaps it was interest in or fascination with the world of rendering, but when Dupps' son followed in his footsteps in rendering sales, the seed germinated and took root.

One of John Jr.'s early clients was the Germantown ferret farm. He was successful in selling the rendering equipment to the ferret farm, but the sale was on credit. When the ferret farm went out of business, the rendering equipment remained unpaid to the Cincinnati Butcher's Supply.

INTEGRITY AND HONESTY

John Jr.'s boss was extremely upset about the loss of payment, which ultimately led to John Jr. leaving Cincinnati Butcher's Supply. With his experience in the rendering business and his knowledge of the bankrupt ferret farm laying idle in Germantown, he and his friend, Robert McTavish (Mac, as he was known), partnered to form a new company, The Germantown Rendering Company.

They bought the rendering plant at a sheriff's auction and Mac moved to Germantown and began running the rendering operation. John Jr. was more interested in building machines than rendering, so he set up a shop in back of the rendering plant to build equipment.

Eventually, John Jr. and Mac repaid the Cincinnati Butcher's Supply the outstanding balance on the rendering equipment. Thus, began the Dupps culture of not letting people down. This became a key to customer service and the resulting loyalty that was instrumental in growing the business.

Dupps' passion for manufacturing (versus selling) led to his selling his share of the Germantown Rendering Company to Mac. He was now free to begin his manufacturing operation as a new company, which he did in 1935, naming it the John J. Dupps Company. His very premature death challenged his son, Jack, to continue the business beginning at the very inexperienced age of 25.

Jack's need for a salesman with an engineering background led to his connection with Frank Schottelkotte, a chemical engineer. Long hours of selling by both men paid off and led to increased demand for their equipment.

RISK TAKING INTO THE UNKNOWN

In the late 1950s came the "Aha" moment in the life of The Dupps Company. It happened when Jack Dupps met Jack Keith, an engineer from Los Angeles. Jack Keith relayed an idea he and another man, Frank Jerome, had conceived to make continuous rendering. Replacing the traditional and much less efficient batch processing with continuous rendering had the potential to revolutionize the entire industry. Jerome needed a source to manufacture the new equipment, and contacted Jack Dupps in Germantown based on the Dupps' reputation for innovation in engineering and manufacturing rendering machinery.

Once the new process was designed and tested, Jack Dupps and Jack Keith patented the process and formed a new company, DUKE, Inc., which stood for their names, "DU" for Dupps and "KE" for Keith.

Another transforming idea emerged in the 1970s. The turnkey concept for the rendering market came into focus. Turnkey enabled rendering companies to enjoy "one-stop shopping" when building new facilities. This potentially saved these companies considerable time, energy, and expense. Dupps parlayed this opportunity into yet another new company, and benefitted from this until the 1980s when market conditions changed. Recognizing market trends, developing products or services to address the trends, and building long-term customer relations in the process is a key part of the Dupps culture.

Another method of finding new markets is old-fashioned trial and error. New ideas spring from ideas gathered by attending industry trade shows, seminars, round tables. The Dupps Company has tried to implement several ideas with varying degrees of success, but has not found its major new market yet. Ideas such as overhauling automatic automobile transmissions on a large scale to sell to automotive dealers and transmission repair centers, and manufacturing high-quality pumps for the environmental treatment industry were tried and abandoned, but not without substantial effort and cost.

The automatic transmission idea consumed four years of Dave Dupps' time. It failed because transmission repair companies and car dealer repair shops make higher profits by applying their own labor and marking up replacement parts than they do by buying complete rebuilt transmissions.

The pump idea was a $2 million investment, although Dupps still makes similar pumps for rendering applications. Two other ideas are still underway, an environmentally friendly dock system for boaters and a class A self storage facility. Both ideas have good reasoning behind them and in Dupps' eyes are worth pursuing. The practice of trial and error is to do the homework, test the idea, and act quickly once it's known if the idea works or not.

Regardless of the product or service idea under consideration, the Dupps formula is consistent: use lots of research, talk at length to the prospective customers, and listen carefully. At the end of the research, talking and listening, make a decision. No one can accuse The Dupps Company of falling prey to the "Ready, Aim, Aim, Aim …" syndrome.

RECIPE NO. 3

FAMILY LEADERSHIP AND MANAGEMENT

Ingredients

- Family members serving as role models for their employees
- Involving family and trusted friends in the business
- Financially and culturally conservative
- Education is important, but must fit people and their desires
- Employee professional development and personal nurturing
- Broad level of communications
- Succession planning

The Dupps' roots extend back in time to John J. Dupps joining the Cincinnati Butcher's Supply Company. He not only succeeded in this business and with this company, but he also served as a role model for his son who also joined the company as a sales rep. John J. Jr. was a man of incredible integrity, and when one of his clients went bankrupt and left a sizable indebtedness to his employer, the Cincinnati Butcher's Supply Company, John Jr.'s life changed.

He ended his employment and struck out on his own in the world of rendering, yet he remembered the debt as if it was his own. When he was able, he repaid that debt.

ENTREPRENEURIAL DRIVE

His interest in rendering equipment led him to the founding of the Germantown Rendering Company with his friend, Mac McTavish. But, his real passion, beyond equipment sales and in the arena of equipment design and manufacturing, led him to found the John J. Dupps Company. Clearly he had family in mind, as he sold his products under the brand name RU JAK, RU named for his daughter, Ruth, and JAK named for his son, John (Jack) Avery Dupps. And, just as clearly he had engaged the interest of his son, John Avery, who took up the mantle of leading the family business at the untimely death of his father.

In 1947, John Avery Dupps made the decision to relocate his family from Cincinnati to Germantown and set up a temporary office in an old rail traction car at the Germantown Rendering Company, which Mac was still running. But, he needed a more permanent structure for the company. Ever the entrepreneur, he persuaded the Germantown Chamber of Commerce to buy an old building in town, formerly the Buckeye Concrete Company, and then sell it to him to be repaid over time. Jack now had his shop and office, but he needed someone to help him build the business. This led to his relationship with Frank Schottelkotte as a lifelong friend and business partner, and the renaming of the company to The Dupps Company.

CONSERVATIVE MANAGEMENT

As the business grew, so also did the need for more manufacturing space. In the early 1950s, Jack invested in a new plant that would ultimately replace the existing operation. On a tight budget and conservative by nature, he bought steel from the old Trolley[3] Repair Shop in nearby Dayton to use as columns and crane runways for the factory. He was demonstrating vision for his businesses' future, provision for longevity through adherence to a tight budget, and innovation as he crafted the structure of his new factory.

Jack's recognition of the potential for continuous rendering was a key to The Dupps Company's future and survival. He also avoided the temptation to "throw the baby out with the bathwater," and continued to serve his longtime batch rendering customers. Using two different companies, he crafted a transition plan that was both simple and effective.

Jack Dupps now had two rendering products that needed his full attention: batch rendering, which continued to be sold by The Dupps Company, and continuous rendering, which would be sold through DUKE Inc. Jack Keith had 50-percent ownership of DUKE Inc., but the responsibility for engineering and manufacturing fell on The Dupps Company and on Jack Dupps for his leadership.

Growing the two businesses required financing, marketing, sales, engineering refinement, manufacturing development, warehousing, and transportation channels. Most importantly, growing the businesses would require Jack Dupps' leadership in Germantown. He recognized his own limitations and the need for qualified help.

GROWTH THROUGH MARKETING AND SALES

Dupps and DUKE Inc. needed a good salesperson, someone who could be on the road to meet with potential buyers, understand their problems and needs, and to sell them products. Coincidentally, the Germantown Rendering Company had gone out of business and Robert McTavish (Mac) was looking for a job. Jack thought McTavish might be a good fit in a sales position because he knew many people in the rendering business and knew the rendering business inside and out, but only the batch system. This was a clear demonstration of Jack's maintaining relationship with someone who had actually been a competitor of sorts in the business. Mac had gone from business partner to competitor and back to business partner with Dupps.

EARNING THE RIGHT TO BE LEADERS

The next generation of Dupps was about to enter the scene. Jack Dupps had six children, four boys and two girls, all of whom had two things in common. First, Dupps was their last name and, second, they all worked at the company in the summers during their teens. They were given jobs such as mowing the lawn, painting lines in the parking lot, cleaning machines in the factory, and performing light duty maintenance. The work experience built character, provided them with some spending money, but, most significantly, gave them a taste of what it would be like working for The Dupps Company full time. Two of Dupps' sons were ready to make that choice: John Avery Jr. (John) and Frank (Hank).

John, the oldest of the brothers, began his Dupps career in 1964 after receiving his chemical engineering degree from the University of Notre Dame. He started in sales and continues to concentrate on sales and business development. When his dad became the chairman of The Dupps Company board of directors, John was named president of the company.

Frank, known as Hank, is a year younger than his brother, John. His dad had visions of Hank attending a four-year college and studying engineering, just as his brother John Avery Jr. had done at Notre Dame. Hank did not care for that idea. He truly wanted to learn engineering, but did not want to take all the other general education courses a four-year degree required. His dad tried to convince Hank that a degree would be best for him and set a meeting with the dean at the University of Dayton thinking that would help. After the dean and Hank spent some time together, the dean told Jack, "Some kids are cut out for college, some want to work in the real world." Dad said, "Okay," and Hank began his Dupps Company career in 1962 working as a supervisor in the factory. Hank worked on his associate degree in industrial technology, he also attended the Hobart Institute of Welding Technology. Hank learned the ropes of the business and is now the executive vice president.

During the rise and fall of turnkey operations at Dupps in the 1970s and 1980s, Jack's youngest son, Dave, was ready to join the company. Dave practically followed directly in Hank's footsteps. He, too, chose to attend two-year college programs that concentrated on his interests in manufacturing and engineering. Dave had a natural intuition for engineering and all things mechanical; that's what he loved. He did not care to devote the time to general courses for a four-year college degree. Dave studied engineering technology at the local joint vocational school and community college. He began his career at Dupps in 1976 working in the shop and became the senior vice president.

The three brothers continue to run The Dupps Company serving the rendering community based on the values they inherited from their father and grandfather: integrity and honesty.

In 1991, Hank's son, Frank, joined the company and shortly thereafter, Hank's other son, Matt, also came to The Dupps Company to begin his career. The fourth generation of Dupps was now onboard. Their education and interests are different. Frank's education is in business while Matt's is in manufacturing, but both brothers preceded their full-time employment by working at Dupps in the summers just as their father and his brothers had before them.

Matt has worked in shipping and receiving, transportation, warehousing, and in the shop. When the company began its latest venture to diversify into the self storage business, Matt volunteered to lead the startup.

Frank has worked in sales and business development. He conceived the idea of getting into the fish rendering market and followed through with research, investigation, and travel to launch Dupps into this new arena.

EFFICIENT AND DURABLE PRODUCTS

Quality and service separate Dupps from the competition. Dupps' competitors do not make equipment that equals the efficiency or durability of Dupps equipment. The competition builds lower-cost equipment, but it does not last as long nor match the performance of Dupps equipment. Dupps is so confident of its equipment's performance that it guarantees a minimal level of output. If the parameters are not met, Dupps will make adjustments or replace equipment until the parameters are met. Hank says, "They (the competition) try to copy our machines, but they don't know the thought and expertise that went into our process design. They end up building lighter and cheaper equipment that doesn't last. We make machines that are sturdier and simpler and built to last."

Even with a Dupps' system or piece of equipment, problems and breakdowns are inevitable. The Dupps Company lives up to its motto: Dupps Won't Let You Down, by providing the best service in the industry. In fact, The Dupps Company service is a model for all industries. Dupps service has four components: a 24/7 customer problem hot line, immediate action to solve customer problems, stocked spare parts warehouses, and free delivery on most spare parts.

CUSTOMER SUPPORT IS THE KEY

Customers have a phone number they can call whenever they have a problem: 24 hours a day, 7 days a week. On the other end of the phone line will be a member of Dupps customer service who will begin immediate action to either ship parts or send a field service person to assist with troubleshooting or repair. Solving the customer's problem is the first priority regardless of anything, including cost. If spare parts are needed, that isn't a problem. Dupps keeps three warehouses with inventory levels sufficient to service customers worldwide. Stock is reviewed annually and adjusted to customers' likely needs for replacement parts. Getting parts to customers is well planned and quick. Dupps maintains its own trucks and drivers who have the experience to advise the customer who needs help. For nonemergency situations, Dupps has regularly scheduled routes, with service people who visit customers in North America every three weeks. They deliver parts at no cost and take parts needing repair back to the Dupps shop for restoration. This level of service has set The Dupps Company far above their competition.

VALUES, LEADERSHIP, AND TITLES

The Dupps Company has a strong culture, ingrained through four generations, based on a foundation of values, leadership, conservatism, employee development, and exceptional customer service.

Integrity and honesty are the cornerstones of Dupps values. They are sincere about taking care of both its employees and its customers. Relentless adherence to core values keeps Dupps on track for meeting its commitments.

Dupps leadership can be described as friendly and loyal, whether it's with employees, customers, or suppliers. The philosophy is to build long-term relationships. With employees, this means being accessible while having high expectations. With customers, it means getting to know their needs and problems. With suppliers, it's making sure there is an equal exchange of services; high-quality purchased components at a fair price. Leadership also means Dupps family members are seen as competent and capable leaders.

At The Dupps Company, a family member must advance through different positions to gain the experience needed to be a corporate leader. Paying one's dues by working in different jobs also gains the respect of the other employees, which is vital for their acceptance as family members.

Titles are only a formality. Family leaders fill positions they feel best fit their interests and skills. John is the president and has responsibilities for business development, administration, and European sales. Hank and Dave serve as vice presidents because they are younger and their passions lie in engineering and production. Major decisions are made by consensus among the brothers after talking through issues. This works best in the long run for The Dupps Company. Titles are left at the door when major decisions need to be made.

Dupps has a conservative culture. Hank Dupps says, "I tend to be a risk taker, but I'm glad we have the conservative culture here." The Dupps leaders don't drag their feet in making day-to-day decisions, but they thoroughly investigate all angles of big decisions. They want to know the ins and outs so that once they make a decision they can feel comfortable with it.

The Dupps Company employees are treated like family and with respect. The Dupps leadership's attitude is to do everything possible to help the employees grow and become more valuable to the company, and then give them increasing degrees of responsibility. This inspires Dupps employees to feel a commitment to their company and to the customer.

TREATING EMPLOYEES RIGHT

Even though Dupps is a company of about 150 employees, its health and wellness programs are representative of a much larger company. Dupps engages a physician who makes a weekly visit to the facility. The physician is available free of charge to the employees and their spouses. The company also provides special medical screening programs, routine prescriptions, and vaccinations. There are special programs available, such as Weight Watchers and smoking cessation. By investing so much to keep their employees healthy, there is less absenteeism and better production. It's a win–win for both the company and the employees. Dupps' wellness programs help to keep all employees healthy and promote excellent attendance. Hank Dupps sums it all up, "Our employees are our biggest assets."

Social programs for the employees foster an added dimension of fellowship and community. These include a family day at a theme park and the annual steak fry where employees grill steaks, and prizes are given to the winners of the games. In addition, there are other benefits for employees.

The benefits and compensation for Dupps employees are above average. Management's strategy is to treat their employees very fairly in both benefits (healthcare, retirement, company physician, medical screenings, etc.) and compensation (annual raises, extremely low lay-off rate, bonuses). This strengthens the bond between the employees and the company, and it shows the employees that the company truly cares for them. In return, the employees are extremely loyal, willing to go the extra mile to meet business goals and to serve the customer, such as sacrificing a weekend to overcome a customer crisis.

The Dupps Company wants to hire people who can do the work and are a good fit for the its culture. Consequently, they use a very rigorous hiring process. For each opening, Human Resources finds several candidates, administers a test to determine if the applicant has the basic knowledge for the job, and then conducts several interviews to identify the best candidate. Dupps makes very few hiring mistakes, and this is demonstrated by a high retention rate.

Dupps prefers to grow employees into key positions rather than to hire fresh employees from outside. A typical person in a key management role might have 10 to 15 years of experience with the company and may have started a Dupps career in the shop and later moved up to supervision. A major advantage of this "internal" approach is that the employee is a known entity, has demonstrated performance, has learned many different skills, can serve in many different positions, thinks more holistically when making decisions, and is steeped in the Dupps core values.

ACTIVE LEADERSHIP

Work is fluid between departments. Employees are expected to not work in a vacuum, but encouraged to seek who they need in other departments by going directly to that person. When an employee has a problem, he is expected to attempt to first solve the problem himself. If he has to go to his manager, he is expected to bring some possible solutions. Working together, they engage the best solution. Hank Dupps believes every employee should be proud of what they are doing. Management encourages employees to solve problems on their own, and even when mistakes are made, the employee feels ownership and pride in his work.

Product development and continuous improvement are ongoing activities at Dupps. Employee teams meet frequently to brainstorm and implement ideas to make work easier, reduce fatigue, improve quality, and reduce costs. The Dupps Company has been doing its own version of Lean for a long time. Numerous manufacturing processes have been improved through the ingenuity of the workers supported by management to make jobs easier to run, improve quality, and shorten turnaround time.

Daily communications is primarily via management by walking around. Seldom are any of the leaders and managers pigeon-holed in their offices. They are where the action is, working on issues, developing plans, implementing, and communicating. They are part of the everyday activities, not isolated in their offices.

Formal communications occur several times a year. Management delivers a "state of the company" address to all employees, generally in quarterly meetings. Topics include future business, new employees, new equipment, backlogs, service awards, employee outings, medical screenings, etc. It's a time when all employees can hear the same message and pose questions directly to top management.

Dupps uses the Annual Business Planning Meeting as a tool to review current position, progress or lack thereof, and to consider future business strategies.

Dupps also has a board of directors composed of the three brothers, John, Hank, and Dave, and three senior executives from outside the processing industry who provide guidance and counseling from a more global perspective. As John says, "Every company should have outside directors to hold senior management accountable." Dupps board members are active businessmen with international business experience who have skill sets and experiences not found within the company. The board also helps the Dupps brothers make major decisions, such as whether to venture into new markets and provides guidance on succession planning.

John and Hank are currently preparing for a less active role in the company. The time has come to pass the leadership baton to others. This is not an easy task, as the name Dupps has so much value to employees, customers, and suppliers. To ensure an efficient transition, the company is going through a methodical process of identifying the next leadership team and the next president. Dupps covets objectivity and, therefore, has selected a succession-planning professional to guide the process. The most important caveat is that the new president knows and understands the company's culture and why it works, understands the industry, and where the industry and company are going.

There is a degree of uncertainty with The Dupps Company's future—the next president—future markets—the new products. However, this much is certain, whatever markets The Dupps Company serve and wherever the Dupps Company name is known, "The Dupps Won't Let You Down."

END NOTES

1. Porkopolis: The nickname given to Cincinnati in the early 1800s when it was the country's chief hog-packing center.
2. Turnkey: A system that is designed, specified, purchased, installed, and started up by a single company.
3. Trolley: A streetcar that runs on rails and is powered by either horse or electricity.

3

Company Story 3—Large Manufacturer

MIDMARK CORPORATION

Midmark is a company whose history is similar to other great American companies yet is unique in its focus, growth, and contribution to creating American jobs. When John Eiting was a member of the board of directors for the Cummings Machine Company in 1915, it had 5,000 square feet of manufacturing space and employed 25 people. Today, four generations later through acquisition and new product development, the company (now called Midmark) has 500,000 square feet of manufacturing space in five locations, employs approximately 1,000 people worldwide and continues to grow. Midmark's growth has been steady and successful and is the result of four major recipes.

1. **Entrepreneurial vision and new product development**
2. **Listening intently to the voice of the customer**
3. **Continuous development of an engaged team culture**
4. **Leadership stability and continuity**

Keeping Your B

The Cummings Machine Company incorporates. It begins producing concrete mixers. J.W. Eiting becomes the first member on the Board of Directors

T
cl
In
a
M
C
th

acquires
Design,
now
cabinets
ntal
nal

Acquires a minority equity position in Janak Healthcare Private Lmtd. a healthcare manufacturer in Mumbai, India . Acquires Progeny®, Inc., located in Illinois, a manufacturer of radiographic imaging products in the human and animal dental markets

1915

)6

2008

1921

2008

2009

The Cummings Machine Company becomes The Industrial Equipment Company and produces mining locomotives, foundry equipment, and custom metal fabrications

L7,

ire

Expands the veterinary product offering by acquiring Sharn Veterinary

Midmark employs over 1,100 worldwide and is headquartered in Versailles, OH Subsidiaries include locations in CA, FL,IL,KY, India, and France

RECIPE NO. 1

ENTREPRENEURIAL VISION AND NEW PRODUCT DEVELOPMENT

Ingredients

- Ability to identify changing market conditions
- Strategy of product diversification
- Develop and manufacture products based on core competencies
- Move into new product markets
- Personal involvement by leadership to support the vision
- Decentralize company and management into product line divisions
- Abandon nonperforming products or products that do not fit
- Grow the business via both acquisition and product development
- Go global

The Cummings Machine Company was founded in 1915 as a manufacturer of cement mixers. By 1921, the company had expanded the product line to mining locomotives, foundry equipment, and custom metal fabrications, and had renamed the company Industrial Equipment Co. Industrial custom metal fabrication and manufacturing foundry equipment became the core business for Cummings for the next 84 years. The stability of the core business and the custom engineering capability allowed the succeeding leaders to try several other businesses in support of change in an evolving marketplace. Many successful companies change their product lines throughout the years by designing new products or buying new companies as market conditions change. The Midmark owners were to demonstrate that a successful and surviving company must have the vision and the management skill to identify the changes along with the persistence to make it happen.

John Eiting was the first family member to be involved with the company from its beginning, serving on the company board of directors and becoming president in 1925. John introduced the strategy for company diversification that continues to this day. John's son, Carl, joined the company in 1930 and became president in 1953. During this period under John and then Carl, the company fabricated such unique products as highway toll booths, electrical control consoles, and the first pressure ladle for the ductile and modular iron industries. The skilled custom engineering and manufacturing supported the core business of mining and foundry equipment, and also served to fund new ventures with the search for growth and diversification.

When Carl's son, Jim, joined the company in 1956, it was time for the company to develop a new strategy of selling products for markets they had not tried. Jim's idea was to shift from the core industrial foundry products and custom metal fabrication to manufacturing products for the more stable and predictable medical industry. Industrial equipment manufacturers historically have to cope with the ups and downs of economic swings with the waste and uncertainty of layoffs and call backs. It was time to move in a different direction, but it also required a vision that would result in success. The corporate strategy was to carefully nurture the core business until the time was right to abandon it.

TURNING POINT

The year 1968 was one of several turning points in the history of the company. By 1968, Jim had convinced Carl to acquire the medical examination table product line of American Metal Furniture Company. The IE Company would never be the same. Carl was not at all sure that this new medical product would succeed. Meanwhile, Jim took to the field in a company El Camino (a half car/half pickup) with a medical examination table in the back, calling on new distributors. To emphasize new and diversified products, the company was renamed in 1967 to IE Industries, which stood for "innovative engineering."

The 20 years following the new direction and the introduction of the new medical products were challenging for the growing company, but also reflect the skill of management leadership in bringing about the change. The foundry and custom fabrication equipment for the industrial markets were the core products entrenched in the know-how and skills of the organization since its inception. However, the new medical equipment product line required a different way of thinking about the new customers and their requirements. In order to develop the medical business quickly, the company knew it would have to acquire new products while at the same time manage the core businesses. As an indication of marketing and sales strength, the company grew 186 percent from 1961 through 1974, for an average annual growth rate of 14.3 percent. The organizational capacity and business focus, as well as the physical plant, would be tested. Jim Eiting knew that the core business would have to carry the financial load for innovation and new product development, subsequently leading to a change in the entire business.[1]

DECENTRALIZATION

For example, in 1974, a critical part of the company's recipe for success was the introduction of the world's only solid frame, hydrostatic trencher used to cut ditches for underground utility lines and general construction. This new product line, from the core industrial business, resulted in IE Industries creating three product divisions aimed at focusing management on three different profit centers. In 1978, IE Industries changed the company name to Midmark Corporation, with three divisions: Midmark Medical, Midmark Power (trencher), and Midmark Steel. This landmark move illustrated that the company needed a divisional management focus for the rapid growth on the way to becoming a new company. Salespeople at first were unhappy with the company name change; however, it was not the company name change that was the milestone, it was the management's focus on the need to decentralize and restructure the company around markets and product lines—continued growth and control of the business required it. The company would benefit greatly in later years from this fundamental change in management structure.

PRODUCT ABANDONMENT BEGINS

Another milestone in management vision and philosophy occurred in 1986 when Jim Eiting sold the trencher business, only 12 years after introducing it. Overall, company sales had increased another 101 percent since 1974, but the trencher power division had not performed as the company had expected. The trencher was a good product designed for durability with little maintenance, but the customer would not pay the price for quality. Besides, a major competitor, Ditch Witch, was already in the market with a less costly product. Recognizing the disappointment in the marketplace for the trencher, in 1986, Midmark sold the trencher line to Bobcat who made a good business from equipment rental. Jim Eiting remarked:

> Failure is without a doubt the greatest learning tool there is … if you cannot recognize and admit mistakes quickly, you are sentencing yourself to a lifetime of failures.[2]

The decision to sell the trencher business was a major milestone and put a series of events in motion that (by 1999) had moved the company from the original core business of 84 years to an entirely new product focus. The Tabbert Stretcher line had been acquired in 1981, the Ritter Medical product line was acquired from Sybron, and the Chick Medical Products acquired from Kirchner in 1986. From 1986 to 1990, sales continued to increase an additional 52 percent. With such continuous growth in the new medical products, the company knew that it needed to make the necessary changes for a new core business. So, around 1990, management introduced several major events that paved the way for a complete transformation of the company:

- A new universal-powered examination table had been in development and was introduced to the market late 1990s.
- Customers required intense education and promotion for the new product, which resulted in a new focus from management.
- The hospital equipment products were discontinued as they required direct sales to hospitals and Midmark's sales channels were through distributors.
- The core foundry equipment business was discontinued.
- The next generation of management was brought into the company.

In 1990, the foundry equipment line was closed, as was the custom manufacturing business just nine years later in 1999. The original core businesses had been replaced by an entirely new direction the company had been preparing for since the inception of the first medical table in 1968. The Midmark recipe for transforming the business was to simultaneously acquire the new medical products while selling off or discontinuing the original core businesses. Midmark owners actually switched over the core business by acquisition and development while staying privately owned and financed. The days of cement mixers and custom foundry products were over.

Peter Drucker, legendary management consultant and writer, has written many times that a strategic part of a company's growth should be in "abandoning" old products and getting out of old businesses when bringing on the new.[3] Few companies take this advice and hang on to old products much too long.

Around 1998, Jim asked his daughter, Anne Eiting Klamar, M.D., the great-granddaughter of John Eiting, to join Midmark. Jim's vision for what was to be 10 years of training and preparation for Anne was like that of the other Eitings before her. She began learning the business from the ground up and later was appointed to the board of directors as secretary. She would go to medical school graduating in 1990, get married, and return to Midmark after practicing medicine as a staff physician at Family Practice Physicians, in Urbana, Ohio. In 1999, she was named vice president and medical director, applying her newly learned medical experience to assure new products being developed would have high clinical utility.

In 1994, Jim Eiting decided to retire after 38 years with the company, and a search was conducted for a new president. Although not an Eiting, the board of directors elected Lou Fisher the next president of Midmark. Fisher was a member of the board at the time.

Midmark began a "growth through acquisition" campaign in 1997, which started in the dental industry with the purchase of Knight Manufacturing. Knight supplemented Midmark's dental offerings of sterilizers, cabinetry, and seating by adding patient chairs, delivery systems, wall cabinets, carts, operating lights, seating, and other accessories.

Going global was Midmark's next venture, and, in 1998, the company acquired Promotal (located in France) to increase the geographical promotion of Midmark's products. Promotal thus became the sales platform of Midmark and Promotal products for Europe, the Middle East, and Africa.

For personal reasons, Fisher left the company in 1999 and Jim Eiting came out of retirement to fill the gap as president until a new president could be found. His daughter, Anne, was one of the candidates for the presidency. Her passion for the business, medical experience, and the fact that she tested highest in leadership and intelligence of any other candidate placed her well among them. The board voted on the candidates and Jim Eiting, who was still a board member, excused himself from the voting to avoid the obvious perception of preferential treatment. Anne was nonetheless selected and in April of 2000 became the fourth-generation Eiting to hold the president's position. In 2003, the board promoted her to CEO.

Anne's passion for Midmark has been no less than previous Eitings, but she has dedicated herself to continuing to grow the company even further. In 2004, Midmark entered the veterinary market, also through several acquisitions. Midmark now was a company that had three separate business units (medical, dental, and veterinary), each with its own leaders, departments, budgets, and goals. The company had learned the value of control through divisionalization in 1978 when the three divisions were originally established with the industrial products.

In 2009, Midmark expanded its global presence by forming an alliance with Janak Healthcare in India. The alliance was intended to synergize the strengths of both companies to be global players. Janak is a leading manufacturer of hospital beds and medical furniture in the Indian healthcare market.

How is Midmark continuing its success today? Since 1999, when Anne was appointed to the company, sales have grown 252 percent or an average of 14 percent per year. Sustaining that growth is a phenomenal achievement as Midmark continues to acquire new companies and develop new dental and veterinarian as well as additional medical products. The answer begins with Midmark's leaders adhering to the company's values of integrity, being customer-centric, teammate development (every employee is called a teammate), and unwavering courage. Anne is at the helm and it is through her leadership that Midmark teammates align and partner to achieve Midmark's vision: "Midmark will be a global leader providing products and services to the healthcare provider, integrating value-added technology for efficient and effective patient care. We will do this because we passionately want to make a positive difference in the practice of healthcare and in every life we touch."

RECIPE NO. 2

LISTENING INTENTLY TO THE VOICE OF THE CUSTOMER

Ingredients

- Visit customers to understand their needs
- Cross functional new product development teams
- Customer centric culture

Midmark was founded in 1915 as a custom manufacturer of industrial products. Providing custom products to the marketplace required direct input from the customer supported by sales and engineering capabilities from Midmark. So, manufacturing to the voice of the customer had been a core competency of Midmark from the beginning. Even the difficult decision to exit the trencher business in 1986 was the result of listening to the customer because of the rejection of the expensive product.

Some 84 years later, the custom industrial products division would be the last original core product to be abandoned. Midmark could then concentrate on developing the medical product capability. The medical products were not entirely custom manufactured and had many standard industry features the customer could use. But Midmark wanted to design medical products to the specific needs of the customer, which was, after all, a continuation of what Midmark had always done. In developing the medical products, engineers of varying disciplines had to spend time at doctor, dentist, and veterinarian offices observing the activities and collecting notes. Subsequently, they would have brainstorming sessions that led to ideas for products or enhancements that made the caregiver's practices easier, more attractive, and more productive.

To differentiate themselves from the standard offerings of many other suppliers, Midmark began an all-out effort to make its products, especially the examination table, the most sought after in the industry. While Midmark had always engaged commercial industrial designers to work with its engineers to design tables that were more attractive and with unique features, a new product development (NPD) team structure was developed that continued this philosophy and included more technical disciplines focused directly on the customer. Most NPD efforts had historically consisted of an engineering manager coordinating the efforts of mechanical engineers on a team, with support pulled on an "as needed" basis from other disciplines. A new structure was put in place in early 2000 that created an autonomous team that was staffed with all of the critical disciplines (mechanical, electrical, software, industrial and tooling engineers, and advanced purchasing agents) with one task in mind: to interpret the customer's unmet needs, develop a solution/product, and integrate it into the manufacturing facility. The first example of this approach was a low-height, power-driven examination table that could rise from patient level, especially wheelchair level, to heights where the physician could perform a variety of examinations, whether seated or standing.

Initially, the new, low-height, powered examination table was a difficult sell to cost-minded physicians. The doctors would say, "I can see the need for accessibility, but I don't have that many patients in wheelchairs." Midmark's marketing department was asked to go to the customer and spend time in physicians' offices observing patients and their interaction with physicians and staff. From these visits, they developed the Barrier-Free® promotion and produced a marketing video for the table.

The video was sent to physicians, informing them that one in five people have some type of disability and would benefit from a height-adjustable, power examination table, including the elderly, expectant mothers, children, obese people, and those with other mobility concerns. The video showed the benefits to the physician's practice of having the powered table, e.g., increased number of patients, increased patient flow, reduced back problems of healthcare workers, better staff utilization, and avoidance of litigation (because the Americans with Disabilities Act requires patients' easy accessibility to examination tables). By listening to the customer's needs and marketing back to the customer, the powered examination table became an overnight success and one of Midmark's top sellers. Midmark's philosophy is that new products do not come from inside the company, but from the minds of the consumer of your product. Midmark develops business relationships with their distributors who sell its product, but new products originate from visiting and understanding the consumer.

Many innovative products resulting from listening to the needs of the customer include products that help dentists make the patient experience more comfortable, e.g., attractive office surroundings and dental chairs that provide heat and massage.

CUSTOMER CENTRIC AT MIDMARK

Midmark is a customer-centric company, which means not only listening to the customer at the customer's workplace, but also providing the customer with the "Midmark Experience." Midmark has developed a customer visitation process where customers are invited to Midmark to observe new products and to learn about the company. The visit is 100-percent personalized and meant to create a lasting impression with the customer. Imagine you are a key customer invited to visit Midmark's headquarters. The corporate jet will pick you up at your local airport, serve a meal en route, and deliver you to the Midmark headquarters. You will have exquisite cuisine at the Inn at Versailles (owned by the company) for lunch. Later, you might have a meeting at Riverwatch (a 20,000-square-foot, timber-framed conference center, also owned by the company), then proceed outside to fish in the stocked ponds or play a game of bocce ball on the lawn. You might be shown the latest products and receive a product demonstration at the customer education center, which replicates a fully equipped doctor's office, dentist's office, and veterinarian's office. Dinner will be at the Inn at Versailles with the finest wine, and, if you were staying overnight, you would stay at either the Inn at Versailles or Riverwatch, both having first-class accommodations. If there is time, you and your host might play a round of golf at the Stillwater Valley Golf Club (also owned by the company).

After all, you are the customer and treated with the utmost respect. The Midmark Experience helps build relationships and endears customers to Midmark. It exemplifies the "Because we care" culture. Midmark has many practices that might be viewed as too expensive by Wall Street standards, but when the practice is analyzed in context with its results, the practice completes the voice of the customer philosophy.

Staying close to the customer has resulted in Midmark providing products of unparalleled value with premium prices the customer is willing to pay. Add the Midmark Production System (MPS), which achieves a three-day lead time capability with extremely low costs and high quality, and Midmark has developed a competitive advantage and a strong market leadership.

RECIPE NO. 3

**CONTINUOUS DEVELOPMENT OF AN ENGAGED
TEAM CULTURE**

Ingredients

- Culture of taking care of those who take care of us
- Company customized version of the Toyota Production System
- Everyone accountable via process and products metrics
- Communication is regular and consistent
- Extensive employee benefits

What is culture? The word culture is often misused by companies to describe some vague change in an organization, but few go on to describe exactly what they mean or intend to do.

> When confronting a new culture, anthropologists start by simply observing how people live. They see many artifacts. They watch how people interact.... Finally, they listen to the people; their questions become a way to get into their subjects' heads and more deeply understand what this community believes and values.[4]

In this context, the Midmark culture is described by those daily activities of management and teammates that show what they do and how they live and work together. Robert "Doc" Hall, Indiana University professor emeritus of operations management, reminds us that top leaders have to take everyone in the same direction in leading the collective behavior, and when necessary lead them in a different direction.[5] He could have been describing the Midmark leadership.

Midmark's culture is modeled after a company slogan that Jim Eiting championed while he was still president. He asked a team from the marketing department to come up with a few words that described Midmark's thoughts and actions toward its teammates, customers, suppliers, and community. The team deliberated at the local pub and thought that if we take care of everyone who takes care of us, then it's a win–win for everyone. The team condensed that thought into three words that has become the core of Midmark's culture: "Because we care," which is every aspect of the business: customer relations, community relations, and teammate relations.

Midmark's direction and focus starts at the board of directors. Anne reports directly to the board. Objectives are set by the board and the strategy is assigned to Anne. Midmark's current top three objectives are centered on globalization, innovation, and people development. The company's daily business activities and improvement projects for the coming year support the board's strategic goals. The entire organization works toward the same company objectives.

In 2002, Midmark began customizing its own version of the Toyota Production System, called the Midmark Production System (MPS), which started in operations, but has spread throughout the entire company. The major goals of MPS is to enrich the employees' work experience and knowledge, reduce costs, improve quality, and shorten lead time.

Midmark's people development occurs from the daily learning experiences of continuous improvement projects and scheduled training activities. The development of the Midmark culture is the development of the teammate learning.

Although an outside consultant was hired for the initial MPS implementation, Midmark teammates have taken on full ownership by developing the MPS department, which serves as a training center and central repository for all MPS materials. As part of the MPS training program, teammates from the entire company are chosen by their managers to train with the MPS leader for six-month periods. This training helps the employees develop MPS and leadership skills. After their training, they return to their departments and are often promoted, as they have developed the MPS experience to implement continuous improvement projects in their departments.

Midmark didn't create the Midmark Production System as a "program of the month" to be often replaced with another program. They created it to support their business needs. For example, when Anne laid out a target to meet a three-day lead time to receive an order, assemble, and ship products to customers, the operations department applied the MPS principles, enabling them to do just that. Their previous lead time was between 3 to 14 weeks. When asked how far along Midmark is with its MPS, the answer is, "We've just begun, and the transformation is a forever journey."

Although MPS was initiated by operations, every department now participates. Departments define their yearly MPS activities by applying Hoshin planning, which involves performing a departmental SWOT (strengths, weaknesses, opportunities, and threats) analysis, three- to five-year departmental goals, and action items to be conducted in the next 12 months. Each business unit executes the actions, charts activities (leading indicators), and the results (lagging indicators). Reviews are held regularly to monitor progress and make adjustments to assure goals are met. For example, one business unit implemented over 400 kaizen improvements aimed at elevating the level of customer service.

ACCOUNTABILITY AND VISUAL CONTROL

Accountability toward achieving the established objectives is assigned to each employee or team who maintain their own performance charts. Charts are everywhere and in every department with topics, such as new product development, personnel development, sales, logistics, customer service, advertising, inventory, engineering, manufacturing, quality, employee bonus, etc. Leading indicator charts plot daily actions, which are indicators of actual goals. Lagging indicator charts show the actual end results.

Production goals are displayed on electronic signs that are updated constantly so the team knows at a glance how they are performing. Charts and signage are everywhere showing problems, corrective actions, trends, locations, identifications, etc. This visual management allows supervisors, managers, and support personnel to know at a glance what is happening in the cell and what needs to be done for the cell to run at peak efficiency. To understand a cell's performance, you simply just go to the cell to view for yourself, relying less on the status of historical reports.

COMMUNICATION

Communication is regular and consistent. Daily team meetings where today's tasks and goals are discussed and compared with yesterday's performance are the norm. Wherever possible, cubicles and partitions have been eliminated to provide line of sight communication and foster teamwork.

Assembly cells are scheduled to takt time (takt time is the ratio of scheduled time available in a shift or a day to customer parts requirements, resulting in the rate at which each part or assembly must be produced to meet customer demand). This allows the mixed model products that have similar characteristics but different assembly times to be assembled in a single cell. Working in a mixed model cell requires cross-trained assemblers and zero changeover times from product to product. The results are a true pull system driven by the customer's requirements, reduced inventory, and accelerated delivery time.

When an assembler in the cell has a problem, he pushes a button that starts a light flashing and music playing from his workstation. This alerts a team leader who owns that song (each team leader has their own song) to go to the workstation, take corrective action, solve the problem, and restore flow.

Materials are brought to the cell by a roving material support person called a water spider (named after the speedy bugs that dart across water) that are constantly retrieving materials from the storage locations and delivering them to assemblers, one by one, in sequence.

Midmark has a vertically integrated operation where many product components are made in the same area. Production orders for components are made from kanban (an inventory control system) replenishment signals, supporting the policy of a visual management across the entire shop.

Financial information is communicated monthly to directors and managers in standard accounting methodology. At the shop level, financial information is communicated in terms the cell members can relate to, such as hours per production, scrap, or rework.

Three times a year, Town Hall meetings are held by Anne and her staff with all teammates in groups of about 100 to discuss the state of the business.

COMPANY PRACTICES

Describing the Midmark daily work activities, the evidence of the work (artifacts) and how people work together leads to a sample of the company practices that have been developed to meet the board's goals, and is a further description of the company culture.

Practice: Two team leaders and one water spider supporting eight production assemblers is normally a high ratio of indirect to direct employees.

> **Result:** Assemblers are not sitting idle waiting for parts, problems are identified and solved, takt time is met, quality is improved, three-day lead time is achieved, customers receive their orders on time, customers are willing to pay a premium price, customer satisfaction and loyalty is achieved.

Practice: Some component parts are made in-house at Midmark rather than outsourced to China or other low-cost suppliers.

> **Result:** Production problems are identified quickly, work in process is kept low, zero shipping costs from overseas, quality can be checked and problems rectified immediately, line of sight visual control, parts are always available to the next process or assembly center.

Practice: The operations team has its own dedicated design engineer and purchasing agent. Normally an operations team would consist only of a production planner, manufacturing engineer, and supervisor.

> **Result:** Problems are identified and engineering changes are made quickly, allowing the manufacturing cells to operate at peak efficiency.

Practice: Taking teammates out of their regular jobs for six months to attend MPS training creates hardships on teammates left behind.

> **Result:** Teammates learn MPS from hands-on experience, develop leadership skills, develop ideas of how to apply MPS to their parent department and implement them when they return. Over time, everyone in the company learns MPS for making improvements in quality, cost, lead-time, and competitive advantage.

Practice: In-house publications and marketing communications department instead of outsourcing the service.

> **Result:** Product teams can have short lead-time and high-quality literature for promotions. Many promotions are

reaching the market space in a short time, sales increase, and growth goals are achieved.

Practice: New product development team consists of mechanical engineer, electrical/electronics engineer, software engineer, and a purchasing agent. The team visits customer sites and conducts studies.

> **Result:** New products are developed quicker and with fewer problems for manufacturing, more new products are provided to the market, market share increases.

Practice: The Midmark experience involves owning a corporate jet, an inn with restaurant, a conference center with lodging for guests, and a golf course.

> **Result:** Visiting customers leave with an experience they will never forget, which makes them feel important and wanting to be part of the Midmark family. Trust is built, product knowledge is gained, orders are placed, and Midmark's goals and vision are realized.

Practice: Teammates are treated with the utmost respect and are considered partners in the business.

> **Result:** For example, the "Feel the H.e.a.t." wellness program (Healthy Engaged Active Teammates) provides teammates with information to keep them healthy through diet and activity. Onsite services are provided either free or at a discounted level and include massages and reflexology services, BMI (body mass index) testing, health risk appraisals (a full body test for which teammates receive extra credit on their insurance), and a variety of other programs. For the mind, the company provides tuition reimbursement, a teammate assistance program, and a mentoring program to help teammates advance to their potential. Midmark promotes and supports teammates affected by tragedy by providing a matching fund for donations raised by the teammates for those in need. There is a profit sharing program that all teammates participate in, and 401K luncheon meetings led by the company's investment group that provide information for teammates' financial planning. The goal is for Midmark's teammates to be dedicated, healthy, engaged, and up to the challenging tasks set before them.

> **RECIPE NO. 4**
>
> **LEADERSHIP AND ACCOUNTABILITY**
> **Ingredients**
>
> - Family members serving as role models for their employees
> - Hand-offs from generation to generation ensures stability
> - Company direction and focus starts at the board of directors

Perhaps the most obvious observation about Midmark's culture is the continuity of almost 100 years of Eiting leadership, beginning with John Eiting in 1915, passing it on to Carl, Jim, and now to Anne. A public-owned company would have had much reorganization in 90 years with changes in management philosophy, changes in direction, trying to satisfy Wall Street with earnings per share, and so on. There seems to be something noteworthy about the leadership hand-off from generation to generation that contributes to the development of the stable Midmark culture. Contrasting the continuity of family leadership at Midmark with frequent management changes at many public companies, the family leadership can offer three stabilizing contributions to an organization. They are "known" for:

- Trust
- Integrity
- Reliability

A family history and behavior of each of its members develops from the many years of growing up, maturing, and doing constructive things in the workplace and community. Family members don't have to ask for a second-hand reference for who they are, at what level of trust they are accountable, what their honesty and integrity level is, or whether they will go the extra mile when the chips are down. Families know that about one another, while it is virtually impossible to know such important details about anyone outside the family, regardless of their work references. It should not, therefore, be surprising to understand why a privately held company such as Midmark has developed the successful management leadership from the people they know, trust, and care about.

Jim Eiting, Anne's father, initiated and developed the medical products business in 1967. He had the courage to strike out in a new direction from the industrial core businesses of mining locomotives, foundry equipment, and custom metal fabrication products. He had the vision to see that the medical products were a stable and growing business, and it was under his direction that the medical products grew into a three-division company for Midmark. Jim also had the courage to abandon the core products to make way for new acquisitions and products developed for the medical markets. He had the leadership skill to change the entire direction of the company. During that period from 1967 to 1999 when the last core product line was abandoned, sales grew a total of 301 percent or an average of 9.4 percent every year. Jim also developed the sales and marketing leader teammates who, in turn built and managed the distributor network, which provided the sales growth and financial health for the company.

Anne Eiting is the current CEO at Midmark. Her leadership style has been described by her employees as open and honest. She is a person who walks the office and shop, talking to her teammates to find out what they need and how they feel about their jobs. She is extremely passionate about the teammates and all aspects of the business. Anne is demanding and driven to make Midmark the best provider of healthcare equipment in the world. She leads by example in everything she does. Anne sets the example for her team to follow. To ensure all executives, managers, and supervisors are on the same page, they are given leadership and human relations training. The leadership program consists of two-day classes attended monthly and takes two years to complete. Anne and her staff were the first to complete the training, once again showing leadership by example.

END NOTES

1. James A. Eiting, "Focus for Success," *Orange Frazer Press*, 2009, p. 50.
2. James A. Eiting, "Focus for Success," *Orange Frazer Press*, 2009, p. 53.
3. Peter Drucker, *"Managing in Time of Great Change,"* (New York: Truman Talley Books/Dutton, 1995, p. 77); *"On the Profession of Management,"* (Cambridge, MA: Harvard Business School Publishing, 1998, p. 75).
4. J. K. Liker and M. Hoseus, *"Toyota Culture: The Heart and Soul of the Toyota Way,"* (New York: McGraw Hill, p. 5).
5. Robert W. Hall, *Target Magazine*, 2009, 5, p. 19.

Section II

Recipes for Success

4

Selecting the Companies for Our Stories

THE PROCESS

With many companies moving operations offshore hoping that lower labor costs would make them more profitable (and with many failures), we knew that there were other companies that kept their operations at home and succeeded. We wanted to find out what made them successful and how others might learn that, with good management, jobs did not always have to be sent overseas for profitability at home. We started with company selection.

The initial cut identified over 350 companies. Each company had to be listed in the top five of their product/industry sector and with 75 percent of their operations in the U.S.A. It was not always possible to judge a company by the profit-and-loss statement because privately owned companies do not publish this information. We included only manufacturing companies because they are complex in their operations and we knew the management process is not simple. Service organizations were excluded from the selection because they can be picked up and moved offshore with relative ease and also moved back again as the Dell Corporation demonstrated. Service organizations do have their own set of problems in moving offshore, but they are not burdened with engineering product design, finding many multiskilled, multicraft personnel offshore, logistics details of shipping and packaging product, finding appropriate factory space, dealing with patent issues and many other problems a manufacturing company faces. Understanding how companies could keep the complexities at home and manage them well was the objective of our company selection.

As we proceeded, we discovered that the successful companies had from just a few to many hundred employees. Perhaps more easily managed we thought, but then they also sold products internationally. We dropped many companies early on because they were already in the process of moving operations offshore and were in a state of flux. Other companies were being sold or had now gone bankrupt. This led to the selection criteria of longevity. As we researched further, we found the best companies had been around for a long time: 50 to 100 years. That was a breakthrough in our evaluation. After all, companies that have been operating successfully for that long must have something going for them.

About 125 companies, such as Hamilton Caster, Dupps, Leupold, Buck Knives, Slinky, American Whistle, AmeriWater, Ferno Washington, REI Outdoor Gear and Midmark, made the first cut. Not all companies wanted to participate in the book nor did they meet all the qualifications. So, we chose Hamilton Caster (102 years old), The Dupps Company (70 years old), and Midmark Corporation (95 years old), each highly successful in their own right and each willing to tell its story.

Many of the companies are privately held, including the three we finally selected. We think the reason may be that the privately held company has a more consistent management succession resulting in a more stable company development strategy than the publicly owned company, which can have a different set of management people every five years or less and, in a 100-year period, that can be destabilizing to success. However, we did not conclude that being privately held is one of the recipes.

5

How We Developed the Recipes

COMBINING RECIPES AND RESULTS

American companies for decades have been searching for the management "silver bullet" for getting out of trouble or for making their organization great. The textbooks are many. We discovered it took several "silver bullets" or recipes from our case studies to find the level of success we were looking for. This is not to say there is a shortage of recipes and ingredients. Our goal was to look for the gold nuggets among the common recipes across the three companies, then the action ingredients in support of each recipe. The ingredients are the action steps that make the recipe work. Without the ingredients, the recipe is just the name of a result. We tried to provide the clear, consistent recipes and ingredients that you could duplicate or integrate into your own company and culture. The single silver bullet is a myth only to be found in the old Lone Ranger days.

What we did find is a lack of understanding of how to combine the various action step ingredients into the right order, steps 1, 2, and 3, and with the right timing for yielding tangible and consistent results. The three successful companies we selected for this book seemed to get it. After our intense evaluation and consistent questioning, it was almost as though they were following a Betty Crocker Cookbook. They each were able to produce and reproduce that tangible result we would see in the Betty Crocker photograph of the completed meal. We discovered how they brought together basic business fundamentals consistently over decades. None of our three companies called these traits *recipes*, but all used similar ingredients achieving like results with their domestic and international markets.

It was our intention to find these ingredients in support of each recipe. Companies like Leupold, Buck Knives, Slinky, and American Whistle, seem to have the ideas. However, most companies have a unique and special culture and product that affects the timing and sequence of their activation of the management ingredients. It was never our intention in our first try to build an all-inclusive cookbook. It was our intention to identify the basic recipes that every successful company stirs up. Maybe later we will add the more advanced recipes like the Toyota Production System or The Distribution System. However, these still require a company to be performing at some level of success with the fundamental recipes in place.

After the first editions of the Betty Crocker Cookbook, you begin seeing sidelines for adding or substituting different ingredients to accommodate differing tastes, styles, and personal dietary requirements. The Betty Crocker Cookbook also provides a list of Dos and Don'ts to help you successfully cook the basic recipe.

So, with that, our intent with this book, and using these three companies as our examples, is first to build a cookbook of the basics. We invite you to see how you are doing against these basics as discovered in the Self Assessment and ingredients of actual examples of American manufacturers that have not only survived the threat from offshore, but have thrived in spite of it.

6

Identifying the Seven Common Recipes

HOW WE DID IT

When we began the study, we weren't sure if there would be common recipes. We thought that from our previous work with companies that leadership and financial control might be common. But even there, the details, or the ingredients, could be different.

We began by visiting all three companies and meeting with the owners and top company leaders. We spent many weeks in different areas of the business asking how work was being done, then observed to verify the results. We examined company histories, old reports, announcements of changes, photographs, previous business plans, and Web sites. With old, successful companies, it was important to segment the company history into linear time lines of important events, such as acquisitions, new product introductions, or company leadership succession. Grouping the history into such categories of change over many decades, started to show patterns that led to the success and sustainment of the enterprise. We discovered that there were common recipes and ingredients between companies even though the names of the ingredient action were not always the same. After sifting the volumes of data and analysis, we identified seven common recipes:

1. Leadership
2. Financial Management
3. Strategy Deployment
4. Continuous Improvement
5. Listen, Learn, Understand, and Act
6. Employee Programs
7. Customer Satisfaction

7

About the Ingredients

MANY ARE COMMON ACROSS COMPANIES

The ingredients for each recipe are what energize or activate the recipe. Leadership, after all, is just the name for a series of management actions that guide organizational activity. Without the ingredients, we wouldn't know what to do or what supported each recipe. As you will see in the next self-assessment section, for each recipe, you will be asked to assess 10 action steps, or ingredients, that you may or may not have implemented in your company. We found other recipes and many more ingredients, but it is the common ones between the three companies that we included in this book.

Pulling the ingredients for success from the many people we interviewed was tedious work. We asked hundreds of people, for example, what the plan of action was for continuous improvement in their area and how did it relate to top management strategy? Out of such questions over the many weeks came the policies, plans, programs, and actions represented by the 10 ingredients of each recipe in the self-assessment. Many of the ingredients are common across other companies, but all of them are present in all three companies researched for this book. We found that all of the associates across the three companies participated in activating the ingredients in their continuous improvement stream. Now, let's move to the self-assessment section so you can answer the question: Now, what do I do and where do I go from here?

We hope that between the stories that tell how they build in America, the self-analysis, and these small hints, you can duplicate, integrate, and begin building your own company *"success stories."*

8

Personal Self-Assessment

The self-assessment of your company with our proven ingredients is the objective of this book. The self-assessment provides you with your own action plan to close the gap from your assessment data. You also may add other success ingredients that are unique to your company.

Here are our top seven recipes and your self-assessment to compare you with the company stories in the book.

1. Leadership
2. Financial Management
3. Strategy Deployment
4. Continuous Improvement
5. Listen, Learn, Understand, and Act
6. Employee Programs
7. Customer Satisfaction

How to take the self-analysis test.

- Score yourself on each recipe's ingredients.
- Assess how well you are performing the ingredients of each recipe.
- Be honest, no guessing.
- Think of examples where you might be doing an ingredient, using a different name, or calling it differently.

RECIPE NO. 1: LEADERSHIP

The process of engaging people to achieve a common outcome. The effective leader leads by example; knows his/her people's desires, strengths, and weaknesses; develops strategies and plans to advance the organization and people; communicates often; is action oriented; has high integrity; and personifies the values of the company.

Score Ratings

0–Not at all	1–Do very little	2–Do sometimes
3–Do often	4–Do a great deal	5–Always

	My Score
1. Our leaders lead by example in every manner from meeting commitments, integrity, social responsibility, respect, sharing the load, and personal work habits.	
2. Our leaders have clear, focused objectives and goals for each department (to ensure business success) and for each employee (to ensure their growth and development).	
3. Our leaders help each department leader and employee translate their objectives and goals into clear, focused direction.	
4. Our leaders walk their areas of responsibility daily gathering data, engaging employees, seeing what their problems are, and helping them develop solutions.	
5. Our leaders take personal ownership for setting direction and making change after collecting data, listening to advisors, and conferring with each other.	
6. Our leaders grow through accepting assignments in different departments and participating in outside leadership training.	
7. Our leaders are selected by a formal board with a succession plan that evaluates all leader candidates on leadership criteria, experiences, and cultural fit.	
8. Our leaders demonstrate the beliefs and values of the company in a way that is genuine and visible.	
9. Our leaders make decisions based on data and metrics rather than on hunches and innuendo.	
10. Our leaders engage the entire workforce in achieving strategic goals via a comprehensive strategy deployment plan (aka Hoshin Kanri).	
My score (divide total by 50, then multiply by 100)	_____ %

RECIPE NO. 2: FINANCIAL MANAGEMENT

The process of controlling the financial metrics and assets of the organization through selected performance indicators (activities and their results) that influence them. Performance indicators are measured more frequently so that corrective action can be taken to bring them into line.

Score Ratings

0–Not at all	1–Do very little	2–Do sometimes
3–Do often	4–Do a great deal	5–Always

	My Score
1. To control our financial metrics, we measure the performance indicators that influence each financial metric, e.g., product cost is influenced by rework, scrap, and work-in-process.	
2. For each financial metric, we have identified all performance indicators that impact it.	
3. We have assigned the department/person responsible for each performance indicator to measure it as frequently as is prudent, e.g., attendance is measured daily by the human resources specialist.	
4. We make the performance indicators visible by posting them openly where everyone can see them. This makes it easy for all employees to see how we are doing.	
5. We have performance indicator charts posted throughout the company: office, shop, and customer service.	
6. Our leaders pay special attention to the charts during their daily walks, gathering data, providing encouragement for maintaining them and asking questions.	
7. We take corrective action when the performance indicators are in the wrong direction for sufficient periods of time. We do not react to incidental changes in direction.	
8. We have a corporate dashboard, visible to all employees, that summarizes the financial metrics and the key performance indicators.	
9. Every employee knows the financial status of the company and what they can do to help make it better.	
10. We have developed partnership relations with our suppliers to ensure metrics for our customers are met.	
My score (divide total by 50, then multiply by 100)	_____ %

RECIPE NO. 3: STRATEGY DEPLOYMENT

The process of generating the strategic goals of the organization and the means of bringing them into reality. Strategy deployment begins with the leaders setting top-level objectives to be achieved in three to five years—asking for input and buy-in by the next levels of management—and assigning tasks throughout the organization to achieve the objectives.

Score Ratings

0–Not at all	1–Do very little	2–Do sometimes
3–Do often	4–Do a great deal	5–Always

	My Score
1. We have a formal strategy to achieve our company's Vision.	
2. Our strategy is formed by performing a SWOT analysis and listening to our advisors and mentors. This tells us what our top-level objectives must be to achieve our Vision.	
3. The top-level objectives are communicated to the next level of management for their input and recommendations. Adjustments are made as necessary.	
4. Each top-level objective is divided into tasks that can be accomplished in the next 12 months and assigned to the employee most able to accomplish it. Management support and oversight is identified.	
5. We hold roundtable meetings with our employees in our "strategy room" to communicate our strategy and top-level objectives with them and to assign them their tasks.	
6. We ensure that the employee who has been assigned the tasks has the skills, ability, understanding, motivation, and time to accomplish the tasks effectively.	
7. The tasks are reviewed frequently with corrective action taken as necessary to keep on track.	
8. Quarterly reviews are performed to determine the effect the tasks are having in accomplishing the top-level objectives. Adjustments and corrections are made if necessary.	
9. Annually, the company's Vision and top-level objectives are reviewed and another SWOT analysis is performed with ensuing current, new, or revised top-level objectives. The process is ongoing and never-ending.	
10. We post our strategy deployment visuals in key areas throughout our company for everyone to see and understand our performance.	
My score (divide total by 50, then multiply by 100)	_____ %

RECIPE NO. 4: CONTINUOUS IMPROVEMENT

The most challenging part of Continuous Improvement is keeping the improvement continuous at all levels of the value stream. The tendency to coast stops momentum and assures eventual decline. Great companies have developed this disciplined culture. Changing the company culture to embrace Continuous Improvement is a key recipe to creating positive outcomes.

Score Ratings

| 0–Not at all | 1–Do very little | 2–Do sometimes |
| 3–Do often | 4–Do a great deal | 5–Always |

	My Score
1. We have a formalized Continuous Improvement program that is led by a full-time employee who is experienced/certified in the various forms of Continuous Improvement.	
2. We train our employees to be the best, support them with coaching, and consider them the basic reasons we have good quality, on time delivery, and exceptional customer commitment.	
3. Our Continuous Improvement program is comprehensive. It includes elements of the Toyota Production System, Lean, Six Sigma, ISO, SPC that we have determined to be helpful to us.	
4. We have written policies and procedures for our Continuous Improvement program that includes a job description, experience and educational requirements, salary range, goals and objectives, and annual review procedure for the Continuous Improvement leader.	
5. Our leaders are visibly engaged in our Continuous Improvement activities.	
6. We have Continuous Improvement activities going on continuously throughout the entire company in the shop, office, and service center.	
7. We have a Continuous Improvement program at our suppliers to improve their performance on product quality, delivery, and cost.	
8. Our leaders are unwavering in leading our Continuous Improvement journey.	
9. We have changed our culture to Continuous Improvement; everyone is involved, trained, and certified.	
10. We foster an environment that encourages problem solving by finding the root cause solutions, discouraging fighting the same fires over and over.	
My score (divide total by 50, then multiply by 100)	_____ %

RECIPE NO. 5: LISTEN, LEARN, UNDERSTAND, AND ACT

Listening is crucial to leaders to learn and understand what is happening and what actions are needed. Good leaders know who to listen to, and have cultivated advisors to fill in their "gaps." Then, when taking action, the good leaders know who to include and involve. The involvement of the key players coupled with the support of leadership is what makes organizations successful.

Score Ratings

0–Not at all	1–Do very little	2–Do sometimes
3–Do often	4–Do a great deal	5–Always

	My Score
1. We have a formal employee involvement program in which we engage our employees' thoughts, ideas, and suggestions, and turn them into actions.	
2. We use a formal employee suggestion process to listen, learn, understand, and take action on what our employees tell us.	
3. We have an interactive employee process that focuses on their training and development needs.	
4. We provide an environment for employees to discuss "their" dreams and personal goals and provide support for achieving them.	
5. We ask every employee to find problems, provide solutions, and participate on teams resolving the problems.	
6. We have a formal supplier partnership program where we define our requirements in quality, cost, and delivery, then listen to their needs and develop a relationship of mutual service, a win–win scenario.	
7. We have a formal program where we go to our customers and observe them using our products, then make improvements.	
8. We have a formal program where we go to the marketplace and observe potential customer needs for the purposes of developing new products and services.	
9. We have a formal program where we learn what our competition is doing with products, services, markets, and cost.	
10. We have an advisory board composed of outside experts who have expertise we lack with whom we meet regularly to discuss economics and market trends, so that we may learn and test new ideas before acting.	
My score (divide total by 50, then multiply by 100)	_____ %

RECIPE NO. 6: EMPLOYEE PROGRAMS

What better way to assure that your employees are healthy, present at work, attentive, well educated, motivated, committed, and endeared to the company than to provide them with resources for the mind, body, spirit, and pocketbook? Wellness programs, tuition refund programs, job rotation programs, profit/gain sharing programs, 401K programs, investment education programs, preretirement programs, recognition programs for promotions, accomplishments, birthdays, anniversaries, births, marriages, deaths, illnesses, and special events will make your employees more dedicated and valuable.

Score Ratings

0–Not at all	1–Do very little	2–Do sometimes
3–Do often	4–Do a great deal	5–Always

	My Score
1. We have a formal fitness program for our employees either onsite or offsite.	
2. We have a smoking cessation program for our employees and their family members.	
3. We have a tuition refund program for our employees.	
4. We have a program to rotate employees to different assignments to broaden their experiences.	
5. We have a 401K plan or other retirement plan for our employees.	
6. We have a profit sharing or similar program that allows our employees to share in profitable times.	
7. We have an attendance bonus program that recognizes and encourages excellent attendance.	
8. We have a "death in the family" bereavement program for employees and their direct family members.	
9. We have an anniversary recognition program for our employees to show appreciation for their commitment to the company.	
10. We have an illnesses support program and a personal distress support program for our employees.	
My score (divide total by 50, then multiply by 100)	_____ %

RECIPE NO. 7: CUSTOMER SATISFACTION

Customer satisfaction before, during, and after the sale is essential to keep your customers coming back. How do *you* like to be treated as a customer? *Before the sale,* do you like to be attended to, treated with respect, given pertinent product information, shown a product demonstration (actual or video), offered a discount or perk? *During the sale,* do you expect the product to function as advertised, sent to the right address, invoiced accurately, instructions that are easy to follow? *After the sale,* would you like a call thanking you for your business, see how the product is working, ask for any suggestions, honor returns or replacements? Of course you would. Any customer would want these, including your own customers. This will make your customers satisfied beyond expectations and will set you on your course to be No. 1 in your marketplace.

Score Ratings

0–Not at all	1–Do very little	2–Do sometimes
3–Do often	4–Do a great deal	5–Always

	My Score
1. We give each prospective customer 100% of our attention and answer every question they have.	
2. We give our prospective customers actual demonstrations or simulated demonstrations via videos.	
3. We offer perks to our customers in various forms, e.g., discounts, shipping, rebates, future purchases, accessories, etc.	
4. We track all our invoices for accuracy of correct price, correct address, etc., and have a corrective action program to ensure we are at least 95 percent accurate on all invoices.	
5. We guarantee that our products function and appear as advertised and offer a product replacement if they do not.	
6. We provide easy-to-follow instructions and/or offer installation services.	
7. We place a personal telephone call to our customers thanking them for their business and asking if everything is okay with their purchase.	
8. We honor our warranties and guarantees in a timely and satisfactory manner.	
9. We offer prompt service after the sale to make repairs and answer questions our customers might have.	
10. We have a sufficient inventory of repair or replacement parts to cover our customers' needs.	
My score (divide total by 50, then multiply by 100)	_____ %

9

Personal Insights and Thoughts

SCORING MYSELF

Now that you have taken the Self-Assessment, spend some time reflecting on how well your company is following the seven core recipes. On the following pages, write the insights and thoughts you are seeing or feeling. List those things you are doing well, those things you are not doing at all, and things you might want to consider.

RECIPE NO. 1: LEADERSHIP

My Score _____%

Insights and thoughts:

Things we are doing well:

Things we are not doing well:

RECIPE NO. 1: LEADERSHIP

Things we are not doing at all:

Things we might want to consider:

RECIPE NO. 2: FINANCIAL MANAGEMENT

My Score ____%

Insights and thoughts:

Things we are doing well:

Things we are not doing well:

RECIPE NO. 2: FINANCIAL MANAGEMENT

Things we are not doing at all:

Things we might want to consider:

RECIPE NO. 3: STRATEGY DEPLOYMENT

My Score _____%

Insights and thoughts:

Things we are doing well:

Things we are not doing well:

RECIPE NO. 3: STRATEGY DEPLOYMENT

Things we are not doing at all:

Things we might want to consider:

───────

RECIPE NO. 4: CONTINUOUS IMPROVEMENT

My Score _____%

Insights and thoughts:

Things we are doing well:

Things we are not doing well:

RECIPE NO. 4: CONTINUOUS IMPROVEMENT

Things we are not doing at all:

Things we might want to consider:

RECIPE NO. 5: LISTEN, LEARN, UNDERSTAND, AND ACT

My Score _____%

Insights and thoughts:

Things we are doing well:

Things we are not doing well:

RECIPE NO. 5: LISTEN, LEARN, UNDERSTAND, AND ACT

Things we are not doing at all:

Things we might want to consider:

RECIPE NO. 6: EMPLOYEE PROGRAMS

My Score _____%

Insights and thoughts:

Things we are doing well:

Things we are not doing well:

RECIPE NO. 6: EMPLOYEE PROGRAMS

Things we are not doing at all:

Things we might want to consider:

___

RECIPE NO. 7: CUSTOMER SATISFACTION

My Score ____%

Insights and thoughts:

Things we are doing well:

Things we are not doing well:

RECIPE NO. 7: CUSTOMER SATISFACTION

Things we are not doing at all:

Things we might want to consider:

10

Next Steps

FOLLOWING THROUGH ON THE SEVEN CORE RECIPES

Your assessment score and thoughts are quite valid from your own point of view, but as with any assessment, the more points of view, the more accurate the data. Your next step is to see how others in your organization feel you are using the seven core recipes. We suggest being strategic about how the data are collected.

Start by having the leadership team, the president, and heads of the various departments take the assessment. Don't try to average the scores because it will be more important to see the differences between the team members. Discuss the differences and try to understand them. At this point, it might be helpful to have a trained facilitator guide the discussion. As a team, develop your collective insights and thoughts, the things you are doing well, not well, and not at all. Then list the things you might consider doing.

The next step is for the department heads to have a similar exercise with their staffs, collecting even more data on how the organization is using the seven core recipes and the gaps they uncover.

Listen, learn, and understand your gaps. Determine what you want to do about closing the gaps, and apply the seven core recipes to secure your work in America or bring it back.

Try following this simple recipe:

Through **Leadership:** Lead by example to move your organization to a new dimension of proficiency and competitiveness by embracing the seven core recipes.

Through **Financial Management:** Develop performance indicators of actions and events that every employee can understand to improve profitability.

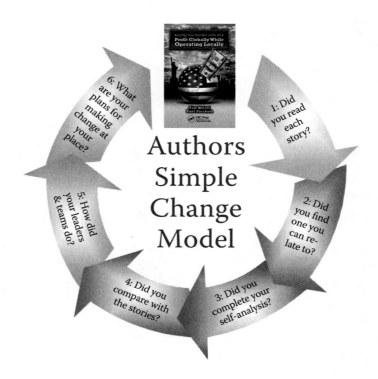

Through **Strategy Deployment:** Set the direction for the next three to five years and engage everyone in the effort to get there.

Through **Continuous Improvement:** Set the bar ever higher for excellence, never being content with the status quo; apply all pertinent Continuous Improvement tools.

Listening to your key constituents: Learn what they are telling you and understand what to do about it. Then simply Act...Act...Act!

The seven core recipes will serve you well. They also will do a great deal for your customers, employees, and your country.

Now, where and what do I do? You just got started. You are now on the track driving toward the next level of success. To sustain your progress, take the self-analysis test annually to see if you are progressing and to evaluate why you may not be progressing. Make it a tool for measuring and sustaining the gains and for continuing the progress. How well am I using the core recipes? How well am I doing implementing them? Also, add the analysis tool with your leadership team or direct reports. Have them take the self-assessment as a personal, self-evaluation, but also use it as a way to improve, make, and sustain positive change.

Then, in three years, see where you have come. One time or one year will not do it. Successful companies make this part of their normal daily work, forever!

SERVICES AVAILABLE

You have read the book, completed the self-assessments, and now if you are looking for support. Where we you go?

The authors can support you through the following organizations.

MainStream Management, LLC

MainStream Management, LLC ("MainStream") is a management consulting firm that provides solutions that create value and drive results for middle-market companies and public sector organizations. Having worked in multiple industries involving a broad set of strategic, operational, and financial challenges, MainStream has worked for some of the most respected individuals, private equity firms, lenders, publicly traded companies, and public sector organizations in the world. Since founded, we have successfully completed engagements in 18 countries across four continents. MainStream has deep experience in the manufacturing, consumer products, government contracting, aviation, defense, printing, industrial products, and food and beverage industries. We are based out of seven offices strategically located throughout the country to serve our clients wherever challenges arise.

MainStream specializes in performance and operations improvement, financial restructuring, strategy planning, interim/crisis management, and transaction services. We assist clients in building business strategies and turning those strategies into everyday work. MainStream's success has extended from operational turnarounds to assisting the best of class with building on its success. Knowing where you want to go is important; knowing how to get there is where MainStream shines. We invite you to learn more about our background, capabilities, engagement results, and leadership team by visiting www.mainstreamllc.com or contacting us at (877) 785-6888.

University of Dayton's Center for Competitive Change

300 College Park
Dayton, Ohio 45469-0186

937-229-4632
www.competitivechange.com

The Center for Competitive Change and our 20+ years of experience in continuous process improvement tools can help you and your organization improve efficiencies, reduce unwanted costs, exceed customer expectations and empower and engage you and your employees to achieve business and operational excellence. Our team is comprised of industry-recognized, leading subject matter experts, actual practitioners, providing unique and customized programs not offered anywhere else in the country except at the University of Dayton. Whether you come to us and attend one of our publicly offered programs or we come to you providing specific, targeted programs or services at your organization, we think you'll be impressed! Check us out at www.competitivechange.com.

LEADERSHIP SERIES

Strategy Deployment (Hoshin Planning)
Project Management for Six Sigma Projects
Leadership Coaching & Mentoring

LEAN SERIES

Introduction to Lean Tools
Metrics (Measures) for a Lean Environment
Human Error Reduction: Root Cause Analysis
Lean Equipment Management: The Foundations of TPM
Lean Equipment Management II: Advanced Reliability Applications
Lean Customer Service-The Key to Quality, Service, New Growth & Profits
Expanding Lean into Your Offices
Managing an Efficient Supply Chain
Toyota Culture Parts I- V

SIX SIGMA SERIES

Six Sigma White Belt
Six Sigma Executive Champion
Six Sigma Yellow Belt
Six Sigma Green Belt
Six Sigma Black Belt

Index

About the Authors

Tim Hutzel, past president of MainStream Consulting, is a 45-year veteran of manufacturing management and industrial psychology. His education and life experiences provide him with the unique ability to blend a BS in engineering technology from Miami University (Ohio) with a master's degree in organization development from Bowling Green State University. The joining of these two disciplines piqued his interests to the point where his research and thesis concentrated on Self-Directed Work Teams. Tim has written and implemented several programs on Self-Directed Work Teams including The Design and Implementation of Self-Directed Work Teams, The Daily Management of Self-Directed Work Teams, and The Supervisor's Role in Self-Directed Work Teams. He also developed the Self-Directed Work Team course for the Association for Quality and Participation.

This blend of the "technical" and "organizational" has provided Tim with the advantage of having a radar screen that goes far beyond the normal scope and toolbox of traditional Lean implementers who focus on kaizen or Lean "events." Although trained by the Shingijutsu experts while he worked in Japan, he discovered that the missing link to sustainment of Lean was the need to treat Lean transformation as an organizational development initiative, not simply a series of Lean events in hopes that the organization would eventually "get it." Tim, who was responsible for Lean at GE Aircraft Engines and on the Jack Welch select team to implement Lean across all of GE, recalls, "Whenever we would ask the Japanese what was next after kaizen they never seemed to understand our need to connect the dots organizationally. I now understand why. Kaizen was only one component of the Toyota Production System (TPS), which began with Japan's reconstruction in the late 1940s. TPS and kaizen evolved over 50 years. The organizational aspect of Lean was always in the background with them as Lean evolved; Shingijutsu never appreciated that we westerners needed to understand that. That was my epiphany—that Lean transformation meant coaching the entire organization to behave in a holistic Lean context, not just the shop floor, not just manufacturing, and not just by conducting Lean events."

Paul Piechota is the executive director for the Center for Competitive Change at the University of Dayton Research Institute. In his positions at UDRI, Paul currently is the principal investigator/project manager for a four-year, multimillion dollar government-sponsored project on performance-based competency mapping. As executive director, he leads the university's outreach center focused on helping companies achieve organizational and operational excellence from leadership team to the shop floor, bank, and healthcare workforce. Paul also held many positions ranging from senior vice president of a small business to concluding a successful 14-year career with NCR that took him from developing and teaching financial systems to top worldwide banking engineers. His career shifted to becoming the senior product engineer for a six-state territory for Texas Instruments Mobility Computing Business Unit. He has had a diversified 26-year career also bringing his early project and process management forward.

Paul has authored of over 30 publications with such titles as *Transforming the Enterprise, Getting to the Future First!*, and *Establishing a Method for Process and Culture Change in the Military.*

Along with being professionally employed, Paul is currently a facilitator for the Dayton President's Forum and active member with the Dayton Tooling and manufacturing Association Workforce Development Committee, Montgomery County Business First Resource Representative, and Dayton Chamber of Commerce Workforce Oversight Committee/ Annual Raj Soin Small Business Innovation Evaluation Team. Other active memberships include Montgomery County Business First, State of Ohio Manufacturing Sector Strategy Committee, Regional Project Management Group, LinkedIn Six Sigma and Lean Groups, and American Society for Quality. Piechota has a BS in marketing from Wright State University and a MA in business performance across global marketplaces from the McGregor School of Management at Antioch College. His PhD program at the University of Dayton is on hold until after the publication of this book.